"I [have] had the upmost pleasure from Ohene Savant. He dares wit[h] knowledge, wisdom, understanding, and talent to transform music into a positive space."

—CHUCK D, HIP-HOP ACTIVIST AND ARTIST FROM THE LEGENDARY GROUP *PUBLIC ENEMY*

"I consider [O'hene] to be an exceptional artist in an interesting age where music and entertainment is concerned... His work is mental and emotional nutrition."

—CHRISTOPHER "PLAY" MARTIN, LEGENDARY ACTOR AND RAPPER FROM THE DUO *KID N' PLAY*

"This man is a genius, he is one of the grand musicians of our time."

—DR. CORNEL WEST, PHILOSOPHER, POLITICAL ACTIVIST, SOCIAL CRITIC, AND AUTHOR

"O'hene Savant is one of the illest producers I've seen in a long time. He's multitalented and deserved to be measured with some of the greatest hip hop producers of our time. His talents are unmatched.... If you're looking for a new experience, O'hene is the one."

—RON LAWRENCE, GRAMMY AWARD WINNING PRODUCER FOR RAKIM, JAY Z, NOTORIOUS B.I.G., COMMON

"In order for [Hip-Hop] music to grow and evolve there has to be those that... think out the box, allowing creativity to be his guide.... That artist's name is OHENE SAVANT."

—CHIP FU, HIP-HOP LEGEND AND INNOVATOR FROM THE GROUP *FU SCHNICKENS*

"We lost James Brown, we lost Michael Jackson, we lost Prince.... I am so grateful that I still have... Stevie Wonder and Ohene Savant."

—CHUBB ROCK, HIP-HOP LEGEND AND RADIO HOST

BECOMING AN EMSEE

The 7 Principles of Rap

O'HENE SAVÁNT

This book is a publication of
Diasporic Africa Press
New York | www.dafricapress.com

Library of Congress Control Number: 2019957171
ISBN-13 978-1-937306-70-0 (pbk.: alk paper)

Special discounts are available for bulk purchases of this book. For more information, please contact us at contact@dafricapress.com.

Diasporic Africa Press uses environmentally friendly book materials, including recycled text paper that is composed of at least 30 percent post-consumer waste, whenever possible.

Printed in the United States of Americaon acid-free paper.

Special Thanks

Eddy Blay

Yaw Prah

Ric Flo

Alex Dionisio

Prada Gee

Sway

Heather B

Tracy G

Geoff Brown

Jason Williams

Feli Nuna

Brockett Parsons

Professor Griff

Phanatik

Dr. Shuaib Meacham

Dr. Tony Anderson

Gee eye zee

Dr. Guthrie Ramsey

T-Lo (The Halls)

Rashaad and Njmah (The Heaths)

Rob Kelly and Lisa Simone Kelly/RèAnna

Mark Batson

Tyhiem "Ty" Cannon

Dr. Dre

Kurtis Blow

Kid N' Play

Reggie Rockstone

Rich Lemaster

TABLE OF
CONTENTS

THE 7 PRINCIPLES

I DECIDED TO start this book with a lesson on the power of the mind because I realize many of you will attempt this art form called rapping or emseeing from a purely technical perspective. Whereas MC (master of ceremony) or emcee are commonly used terms for a rapper, I prefer *emsee* because it implies a "master of vision," the goal for any artist on the mic. However, in some instances in the book, I will use *emsee* and *emcee* interchangeably. The technical approach to emceeing will get you far, but emseeing will take you to the unknown and unexplored regions of creativity and artistry.

Everything, and I mean everything, that I've innovated as an *emsee* was precisely because I was able to *see* it and because I believed I could accomplish it. Now, this exploratory process happens in stages. First, you must think it could be possible and then you must believe it is possible. Finally, you must know it will happen. Being an emsee is about having vision—seeing the unseen and hearing the unheard. You must be able to see into the future and imagine what you are trying to accomplish, as if it already happened. Imagine it to the extent that you are riding around in a car, listening to it. Or, you are somewhere walking and playing it in your headphones.

The larger lesson you should take away from being an emsee is this: you can do anything you set your mind to, but you can also become what you imagine. This may sound like some pep talk from a self-help guru, but this is as real as the air we breathe.

Everything you will accomplish starts in your mind. In fact, you can't even move without first thinking about it. Before you pick up a utensil to eat, there is the thought to do so. The emsee must train his/her mind to go a step further. Most of us only use our minds to do immediate things. Things that are right in front of us. If we project our minds into the future, we can bend time. Similarly, we can access the past if we project our minds there.

This may seem unusual, coming from a rapper, but I've never approached rap as just a rapper. I have always imagined possibilities, and these possibilities are sometimes found in the past or in the future. Your mind will be your most valuable asset as an emsee. Your mind and heart, I should add.

Many of us think our minds are in our heads. Yes, that's where our brain is located, but thinking our mind is our brain is a limitation. Thinking that way automatically gives your mind boundaries. What if I told you your mind was everywhere? For example, your mind is here with me. Or, your mind is at your best friend's house, or the grocery store in your neighborhood right now. Notice your mind focusing on the places I say your mind is. Notice how your mind can move around and how fast it happened. Therefore, we should not limit the power of our mind by assigning it a location. The mind is everywhere—everywhere and nowhere at once. You need to *see* everything you are going to execute as a rapper or emsee.

I want you to become familiar with seeing words, seeing your performance before it happens. The rapper, Blind Fury, may lack natural sight, but he is an emsee. He can see lyrics in a way most cannot because sight is not just about the physical eye. As an emsee, I want you to approach the techniques I will share in this book with confidence. The confidence necessary to learn these principles I'll share, and the confidence to master them. The only thing I ask for these priceless lessons is that you pay if forward and teach future generations the art of being an emsee.

I thank you for choosing this book and the lessons that await you; I'm sure you will learn something from them. This book was a true labor of love. First, a love for you, the learner, and secondly, a love for rap and Hip Hop. The world of emsees is a world onto itself. The examples used in this book are not the only examples of greatness in this universal art form; there are more. These were just the ones I felt the need to use for this project, while attempting to be as objective and open-minded as possible. I also want this book to be intuitive and accessible, and so I've tried to simplify the complex. I call this *simplexity*, for emceeing is not about rapping with the most words but finding the right words and delivering these words effectively.

THE POWER OF WORDS

THERE IS POWER in words and word sounds. As an emsee, your greatest asset—other than your mind—will be words. They work hand in hand. When you rap, you are literally sending sounds (energy) into the atmosphere. The words travel and continue to exist even after you are long gone. Now, I don't mean this in a poetic sense. Your words, literally, never die. The first law of thermodynamics, also known as Law of Conservation of Energy, states that energy can neither be created nor destroyed; energy can only be transferred or changed from one form to another. In other words, words are sounds and sound waves are energy. Energy travels through the air on particles and enters our bodies through the ear canal. Not only does the sound enter our bodies, it travels into the universe and affects the environment. Sound can cure and inflict harm; for example, did you know that sound is used in military warfare to disrupt the enemy's mental state and there are weapons that guide sound pressure to be shot at foes the way bullets work? Yes, sound guns! Sound is guided in hospitals to break kidney stones with Shock Wave Lithotripsy, and sound (music) is also used to help the autistic communicate because music stimulates both hemispheres of the brain.

Beyond simply rapping, I want you to understand the power of words in your own life. Over the years, I have developed mantras. Mantras that have helped shape my mind which in turn has improved my craft and overall life. The mind *is* your most valuable asset and words have the ability not only to shape other people's minds, but yours as well. Rappers have known this for some time now. And so, begin telling yourself that you are great, that you are the best, that you are number one, and a master of your craft. This is neither delusional, egotistical or even narcissistic. That belief in your mind, in yourself, has nothing to do with ego. Your mind must be trained to embrace the greatness you are becoming as an emsee. This principle and belief apply to rap, but it can also be used in any discipline. The sounds made possible through emseeing has power, and it is a power to uplift and enlighten those within and outside of the Hip Hop world.

WHAT IS HIP HOP?

A DIVERSE PANEL will undoubtedly produce a range of responses: the breakers call it dance music, pop radio labels it trap, KRS-One calls it "boom bap." While it's important to focus on aspects we hear on the radio, that's only one part of Hip Hop. Technically speaking, the musical aspect is rap. And while rap is the focus of this book, it's important that we begin by talking about what Hip Hop is and from where rap comes.

Hip Hop is an expressive cultural package, an umbrella term with several forms. You may be familiar with the argument that Hip Hop is not really a culture, but a subculture. I take some issue with that notion. Let's look at what culture generally means, so we can determine whether or how Hip Hop qualifies. Among several dictionary definitions, culture refers to a "set of values" or "social practices associated with a particular field, activity, or societal characteristic." Each element in this definition suggests Hip Hop is part of African diasporic and urban cultures out of which it grew but offers a distinctive "set of values" and "social practices" in the "particular field" of expressive culture.

Hip Hop is also an international movement. Members of our group are easily identifiable. If you catch the R train to Madison Square Garden, the M-6 to Madrid's Real Jardín Botánico Alfonso XIII, or the Ghanaian *trotro* to Nation Theater, you can always tell who is going to see the pop rapper of the day or the artist who has a cult following. As an expressive culture, we in Hip Hop have created our own distinctive approach to style of dress, language, style of music, and all the other trappings of a cultural phenomenon. And one of the most identifiable parts of Hip Hop is the music, more specifically rap.

For a second, let me take you back in time. This is how the story of Hip Hop was conveyed to me. In the early seventies, people are in the dance clubs in New York City and they're listening to their favorite James Brown and disco records. Back then, of course, they used turntables, the only medium at the time. Imagine not Serrato, but only basic play and stop options.

These DJs are spinning the most popular records of the day. It's an enjoyable experience. Though these songs with lyrics made you dance, breakers (b-boys and b-girls) were looking for something more open. Eventually, DJs would reach that part of the recording we now know as the *break*. Here, the vocalist typically takes a break and the emphasis shifts to the instrumentation. This is also called the *bridge* or the *vamp*. DJs noticed this part of the song dramatically shifted the energy in the room, but the day's technology limited their ability to act on the observation. Again, the turntables could only play or stop.

The genius of these pioneers of Hip Hop was that they figured out a way to take this break and extend it, by bringing in another turntable. Imagine two basic, old-school record players in proximity and feeding into the same speaker system; routine now, but non-existent at the time. With these record players side by side, DJs would start the first turntable, play the loop all the way until the end. Moments before the break concluded, they would begin the same loop from another copy of the same record on the second turntable, but this time beginning at the break. In other words, when the beat ended on the first turntable, it began on the other turntable and DJs had to juggle between instrumentals to keep the beat going.

It is important to note DJs had accomplished these feats without the manufacturers of record players anticipating this use. As the art form became popular, record players would evolve into "turntables" throughout the 1980s and 90s. Then, DJs who missed the beginning of the break by just a second or two could simply pull the record back with their fingers, whereas the pioneers had the lift the needle and begin anew. Eventually, turntables would allow for multiple outputs so a DJ could listen to record number two through headphones while record number one entertained the audience. This advancement allowed DJs to perfectly time the exact or optimal moment to switch between records so the break could play without "skipping a beat" (also giving rise to the colloquial saying, which meant completing a task with perfect timing). Modern DJs make this process seem flawless with the aid of technology. Today, we can grab these breaks from an electronic file of the song and, with the right software, produce infinite copies to simulate old-school looping.

We have become so accustomed to this process. It may be difficult to imagine the early days, so allow me this analogy: those of us that joined Twitter in 2007 may recall a lot of the functionality we enjoy today was invented by the users. Today, sharing someone else's tweet with our followers is as simple as pressing the Retweet button. However, in the beginning, we needed to copy and paste the original tweet, then type the word "Retweet" (eventually "RT") along with the person's username. If the original tweet, plus the word "retweet" and the username no longer fit within the character limit, we had to take creative license with acronyms and misspellings, typing "b4" instead of "before" or referring to my 2006 album *Inner City Soul* as "ICS." It was clunky and often an imperfect experience, but we were so enthralled with the innovation, none of us seemed to mind.

Ultimately, the practice of looping breakbeats became recognized as not only a derivative of the original song, but a form of art itself. Designed to facilitate dance, the dancing also soon evolved, and breakdancing ("dancing to the break") was born. Now this is not to say that the specific body movements in breakdancing started at this moment. There are many who point all the way back to pre-industrial Africa for its origins. If you observe the martial arts style *capoeira* from Brazil, you'll see a lot of the movements used in breakdancing, making it clear these two art forms have a common ancestor.

As for emceeing, I can imagine this is how it came into play: at some point, there's a guy, not the DJ initially, but a guy who's standing next to the DJ, thinking, "Man, I wanna say something while the crowd is going crazy." So, this person grabs a microphone, connects it to the same speakers, and says something like, "Now everybody in the place to be, put your hands up and rock wit' me" or something similar to get the audience involved. He would have said it rhythmically to not disturb the flow of the music. In addition, phrasing had to be clever in order to earn the audience's admiration and encouragement to continue. Eventually, the vocalist earns more notice; club goers anticipate his involvement. Within the history of Hip Hop, that guy is my ancestor, the first emcee, the first rapper.

This is the Hip Hop iteration of a rapper or, as it is called in Hip Hop, the MC or emcee. Specifically, Grand Master Melle Mel is the first emcee (properly credited as the first to use the term "MC" to describe the rhythmic, rhyming vocalist that now accompanied DJing). However, there is a tradition of rapping that goes all the way back to the jazz era, and before that, what was initially called the rapping DJ and further still the griots or *jeliw* of West Africa.

Douglas "Jocko" Henderson is known to have rapped on his radio show *The Rocketship* on WDAS, WOV, WADO and WHAT (the latter two were both broadcasted in the New York area in the 1950s and 60s). Growing up around this time were most of the pioneers of the Hip Hop movement. Rap was not only a popular artform before it became solely associated with Hip Hop, but it was an established discipline as well. One of the best things I can give you is a love and appreciation for those who came before us. This is a sign of a true emsee. In a 2002 interview, the highly intellectual emsee and producer Odisee said that funk legend Gary Shider was one of his biggest influences and encouraged him to do music in the studio, and A Tribe called Quest was his biggest influence as a Hip-Hop artist. Invoking your influences is a way of honoring their contributions to your life and career and it is important to do because it gives the next generation of artists/emsees a road map, so they can take the artform further.

Some of the pioneers of modern rap who inspired what we call Hip Hop include the Jubalairs, a 1930s-to-50s gospel and soul group that incorporated rap in their songs with soulful harmonizing as background music. Among the legendary radio jocks, we have Douglas "Jocko" Henderson, the multitalented Pigmeat Markham who, on the song "Who got the number," raps in such an advanced way in 1969 in that he and his rap partner had a back and forth song structure. We can't forget The Last Poets, James Brown (the Godfather of soul), and Radio personality Jack the Rapper. These are the forefathers, the foundation, of the expressive culture we now know as Hip Hop, and they should be honored for their contributions.

I covered this history briefly to paid homage but also because, in this book and artistically, I am seeking to establish rap outside of the confines of Hip Hop. This is important because I have always viewed rap as the vehicle and not the destination. Hip Hop is the destination, but not the only destination. Having this mindset will allow you to be genre-less in your approach as an emsee. Being open to the idea that rap can musically go anywhere, from Bebop to Western, classical, blues, country, Hi-life, House, Reggae, and so on. In addition, rap can lyrically go anywhere. When it comes to the subject matter, rap is as diverse as the world we live in.

People rap from their perspectives and experiences and at times even rap from the perspectives of others. Throughout my life, I have experienced rap from all walks of life. Everything from

Christian rap with The Cross Movement to atheist rap with Greydon Square. There's an entire *battle rap* movement based around a-cappella rap with artists such as Daylyt and Illmac. There's even a genre called nerd core where the subject is video games with artists like Mega Ran and MC Frontalot. Rap is a medium and so there are rappers from all over the world. From the U.K. with artists like Sway Dasafo to Ghana with artists like Teephlow and AJ Nelson.

I couldn't accomplish the mindset that rap can be genre-less, that Hip Hop is the destination, by simply being knowledgeable about the pioneers. My knowledge of the pioneers helped to serve as the algorithm for this mindset, because they are the beginning, the foundation of Hip Hop. And today, through them, we commonly recognize Hip Hop's five basic elements: Emceeing, Deejaying, Beatboxing, Breakdancing, and Graffiti art. Our focus in this book is the first element, Emceeing or Emseeing, broken down into seven principles: rhymes, composition, wit, word manipulation, voicing, flow, and live performance.

RHYMES

> Rule: Learn to hear similarities in words. Many words are related in sound. Learn to hear the similarities effortlessly

ARHYME IS DEFINED as the correspondence of sound between words or the endings of words, especially when these are used at the ends of lines of poetry.

The reason you are reading this book is because you want to know about rap, rhythm, and poetry. But before we get to the rhyme aspect of rap, let's review some basic elements of production. You can no more rap on a beat without a foundation in production than you can drive safely without a basic awareness of the road. The following exercise is a breakdown, set to the Hip Hop classic, "You Know I Got Soul," by Eric B. & Rakim:

1. Search online or through your collection to find this classic, then listen to it. Concentrate on the low thud you hear in the background. This is the "kick" or the bass drum. On a drum set, you normally see someone

using their foot to depress a pedal that triggers a mallet which strikes the large drum (on the floor).

2. Next, focus on the higher-pitched short note that resembles a lone clap in a narrow hallway. This is the snare or snare drum, which in popular music you may have heard variations of. The snare is that part of the drum-set, typically found on the left side of the drum-kit. It is the higher-pitched drum that is found in between a tom-tom drum and the kick (or bass drum) on the floor with the hi hat to its left (for right-handed drummers). Of course, there are different snares. Drum machines, more popular in rap, have a variety of timbres (textures). For example, southern-based rap like *crunk* and *trap* uses 808 snares, which originate from the Roland TR 808, thus the name. In short, the kick and snare drums work hand in hand. Their relationship and your ability to identify the kick and the snare is important if you want to rap.

3. Finally, for a simple exercise, try this: Practice steps one and two with different songs, and see if you can isolate the kick and the snare.

Now that we have a common understanding of these beat elements, let's move on to rhymes. First, we'll focus on external rhymes, then internal rhymes.

EXTERNAL RHYMES

EXTERNAL RHYMES ARE when the rhyme is at the end of the sentence. On the 1987 song "I Need Love," the legend LL Cool J says:

> *When I'm alone in my room I sit and stare at the* WALL
> *And in the back of my mind I hear my conscience* CALL

Consider also Grand Master Caz from the legendary Cold Crush brothers, when he says:

> *I DJ'ed in house parties, with BSR's*
> *Transportation for my set? Two or three* CARS
> *Carried amps in the rain, speakers in the* SNOW
> *Spent more than I made when I did a* SHOW

Both used a style of rhyming that is the foundation of the rhyme structure. Later rappers built upon this foundation with external rhymes. Here's another, foundational example:

> *My name is O, I'm here to* SAY
> *I rock to the beat like every* DAY

Here, "say" and "day" are the only rhyming words and they fall at the end of each line. This example and those from LL Cool J and Grand Master Caz are all external rhymes. You hear this kind of rhyming frequently in older rap songs from the late 1970s and early 1980s. The earliest recorded rap used this method of rapping. It is the least complicated method of rhyming. In order to execute this style, you simply need to think of words that sound alike. Focus on the middle of the word, or the vowel sound. When you hear the word "look," words like book and cook come to mind. These are obvious and easy choices, but they tie into the universe we'll explore in a separate topic called Assonance. For now, let's turn to internal rhymes.

INTERNAL RHYMES

INTERNAL RHYMES ARE those that show up in the middle of a bar or sentence. Hip Hop legend and genius Rakim popularized this approach in the late 1980s, although it should be noted Kool Moe Dee, Grand Master Melle Mel, and Grand Master Caz all previously used internal rhyme. Rakim's contribution was an evolution of this style. One of the lesser known contributions of Rakim was the dramatic shift in his cadence that made rap more conversational as well as his rhythmic timing, which he has said was inspired by Bebop music, specifically saxophonist John Coltrane. In "I Ain't No Joke," Rakim raps:

> *When I'm* GONE *no one gets* ON *because I won't let*
> *Nobody* PRESS UP *and* MESS UP *the scene I set*

In the first line, notice that "gone" rhymes with "on," and, in the second line, "press up" rhymes with "mess up."

Big Daddy Kane has since improved and evolved his style but

in 1988, he was a master of the internal rhyme flow. Take this section from his 1988 song "Raw":

The rhymes I USE *definitely a*MUSE *better than Dynasty and*
Hill street BLUES
I'm SURE *to* SCORE *a*DORED *for* MORE *without a* FLAW
cause I get RAW

Note that "flaw" and "raw" are both pronounced like score. This could be the result of Kane's New York accent, but I wouldn't be surprised if it was the genius of Kane's understanding of vowels and the concept of assonance.

The easiest way to use the internal rhyme method would be to look for words that sound like other words. The more unique sounding words will be more difficult to create rhyme schemes, but as an emsee, you should always be able to create something out of nothing. Start with simple utterances: open your mouth and speak sounds, specifically vowel sounds, then add consonant sounds to the vowel sound spoken. Take the word Sound, replace the S in Sound with other consonants in alphabetical order, and begin with Bound, Cound, Dound (which could become **downed**), Found, etc., until you find the words you need. When you do this, match the sounds that you are saying (invented or not) with actual words that have meanings. Try this exercise without resorting to the Internet or a rhyming dictionary. When you can find many words that rhyme with your utterances, you have something with which to build an internal rhyme scheme and to compose a rap.

2
COMPOSITION

Rule: Learn the art of organizing and structuring your ideas in rap. Art has no boundaries and so these are guidelines. Learn the guidelines as a point of reference

CRUCIAL TO ORGANIZING and giving structure to your ideas in a rap is knowing how to count bars, the purpose of hooks, the difference between written and mental composition, the two types of freestyles ("off the top of head") and the art of storytelling. We'll start with how to count bars.

HOW TO COUNT BARS

COUNTING BARS IS very simple. A bar or measure has 4 counts, and since one line of lyrics equal one count, there are four lines of lyrics in a bar. Each bar usually has the same number of beats in it and so each bar with only four beats is in 4/4 time signature. Most rap, in fact most popular music, is in 4/4 time signature. This means, once more, you have four beats per bar. When looking at a digital audio workstation, the thing moving across the screen is called a marker, and that is what we use to count. However, whatever it is you are using to keep time in the future, just know that you are looking for what is the equivalent of a metronome. And that the time (if in 4/4 time) must get all the way to "five" to represent the end of the fourth beat. For example, count:

One, two, three, four (FIVE) is one bar or measure.

One, two, three, four (FIVE) are two bars or measures
One, two, three, four (FIVE) are three bars or measures.
One, two, three, four (FIVE) are four bars or measures.

(Listen for the fifth count as another bar after each cycle)

And that's four bars. With very little practice, it will quickly begin to feel natural. It's so rhythmic, everyone from LL Cool J to K-Os have used this count for a hook. Now, I want to extend this and take you to sixteen bars. There are sixteen bars in a verse in most rap songs and so this time we'll count to the seventeen to reach the end of the sixteenth bar. Let's count:

One, two, three, four
One, two, three, four
One, two, three, four (that's three bars)
One, two, three, four
One, two, three, four (that's six bars)
One, two, three, four
One, two, three, four
One, two, three, four
One, two, three, four (that's nine bars)
One, two, three, four

> One, two, three, four
> One, two, three, four
> One, two, three, four
> One, two, three, four (almost there)
> One, two, three, four
> One, two, three, four.

And that's sixteen bars. You would have to get all the way through the full measure to get the full bar. Having this essential background in rhythm, we'll move on to lyricism.

HOOKS

THE FOUNDATION OF good rap writing often revolves around the *hook*. The hook is the catchy part of the song that you hear repeated several times. It repeats itself as an invitation for the listener to join in. The hook is important because it's the thing that makes the song catchy, some would say infectious. The moniker "hook" perhaps even derives from this catchiness or infectiousness, because it "hooks" us. I'll give you an example. If you check out my song "I Rize Above," you'll hear this hook:

> *Yeah*
> *I, I rise above*
> *All of your hate and your lack of love*
> *See I rise above and y'all can stop me*
> *I rise above. So go ahead and watch me again*
> *I, I rise above all*
> *All of your hate and your lack of love*

See I rise above and y'all can't stop me
I rise above. So go ahead and watch me now

You'll notice this hook is repeated throughout the song. Read the hook one more time, then look away from this page and try to remember as much as you can. How much were you able to recall?

Hooks of this type are purposefully repetitive; I say "rise" six times. They also focus on simple concepts that make a song easier to remember. All this adds to the enjoyment of the song. Every day, our brains take in a lot of information, and it constantly strives to simplify and organize this information. The brain therefore appreciates a catchy hook simplifying and organizing this information for us. Our brain, in turn, prioritizes this information (as in, the best way to understand heartache is through our favorite break-up song, not a five-hundred-page psychology textbook) and we interpret this prioritization as enjoyment.

Alas, as effective as this is, it's not the only way to approach hook development. I've developed a few terms to break down the different approaches to rap hooks. Above, I referred to a stanza-type chorus. Stanza in that it's like a short verse. Most traditional rap songs contain three sixteen-bar verses and a four-bar hook, which can consist of one bar repeated four times or two bars repeated twice, following each verse. Occasionally, this hook also opens the song or is repeated four times to close the song and functions almost as a fourth verse.

Alternatively, a rap song may have a melodic-type chorus. In the melodic-type chorus, the hook resembles an R&B chorus, where the bars are sung. Rappers that are also able to hold a note such as J Cole, Chance the Rapper, K-Os, Chamillionaire, or Andre 3000, will often sing the melodic chorus themselves. Others may collaborate with a more skilled singer. Some singers, dubbed "Hip Hop singers," like Nate Dogg or Frank Ocean, made a name for themselves writing and singing hooks on popular rap songs. Finally, some rap hooks, in lieu of a live singer, feature a sample of an R&B record from yesteryear.

My song "Just Another Day" features my brother and singer Greg Stamper Jr. Earlier tracks, such as "Login Out" and "My Apology" from the *Inner City Soul* LP featured Sheda. There are so many songs we've done with melodic choruses, including, for instance, "Silence in the Morning" with singer Joe little from the *A Lack of Convention* LP. After each verse, the singer sings a melody, hence "melodic-type."

When I taught at Temple University, a student brought to my attention choruses consisting of record scratching. This is a type of hook or chorus where the DJ scratches and mixes between verses. DJ Premier made this technique famous. Along those same lines, some rap hooks also consist of beatboxing, scatting, instrumental solos, or prose. We will lump all of these into the category of Freeform hooks.

The art form, of course, continues to evolve. Rappers, DJs, and producers continue to invent new types of hooks. A movement out of Houston lead by DJ Screw created Chop n' Screw. Here, a short phrase (either original lyrics or sampled) is slowed down and repeated using technology and words are broken in half to simulate a kind of robotic stutter. Standing on their shoulders, I did my own version of this style in the song "DM" for the *A Lack of Convention* LP.

Finally, one of the earliest and still most effective is the "call and response" hook. Throughout the 1980s, concerts would frequently employ this method (even when it was not a part of the recording). To hype the crowd, the rapper(s) would say,

When I say X, you say Y

I've done this myself, instructing people at my shows:

When I say, Oh, you say Hene
Oh
   Hene
Oh
   Hene

Each style of hooks has its own merit. The call and response style work best in live performances. The melodic type has crossover appeal as fans of both the rapper and singer may find the song attractive. I've found that freeform hooks attract more Hip-Hop aficionados, fans that like to analyze music, so anything creative and non-traditional catches their ears. Carefully consider your target audience when deciding which type of hook to use. Having developed the skill of hook creation, let's talk about verse composition, looking at some basic methods for composing a verse.

WRITTEN COMPOSITION

THE FIRST APPROACH is the written method of composition. It is the most common form of composing raps. Writing is a great way of keeping track of ideas. There are many times where I will just write down some simple thoughts or punchlines, sometimes even phrases. The written method has advantages and disadvantages.

Some of the advantages of writing your lyrics are that no matter how long ago you've written them, you'll have them, unless there's a fire or some other unfortunate event. Written lyrics also gives you a great view of everything happening in a verse. You're able to zoom in on every detail and go over it, making changes in a way that could improve your verse, especially when you are aiming for complexity.

Some disadvantages of writing your rap is that you run the risk of becoming dependent on seeing your raps in front of you for a performance. For the emsee, this is not the best use of your mind's eye and ear. Recording in the studio and reading from a paper or device doesn't translate well on recordings because it sounds like you are reading. Reading is typically done looking down, but the way to fix this is simple. Hold the paper (or device) from which you are reading up, so that you are looking up to read. This will create the illusion that you are performing something you've memorized. The reason you need to do this is simple: the normal way to read is to have your head down. Think of public speaking. If you went to hear a speaker, and the speaker spoke with his or her head down, would you think the person was confident?

No. Speaking with your head down in any setting is considered timid—the opposite of the confidence you want to exhibit. The goal of the public speaker is to project confidence. The goal of the emsee is to *be* confident, and so simply holding the paper or device upward (with your arm extended outwards) will make a huge difference.

As an exercise for written compositions, begin writing down your thoughts. You can start with rhyme and rhyme schemes. For example,

Chair/stair/air/heir/
Flow/go/low/

These are very basic ideas, but the point is to begin practicing written rhymes, looking at them, and dissect words as a discipline. This exercise will prepare you for mental composition.

MENTAL COMPOSITION

ANOTHER METHOD OF composition is a mentally composed verse or "a mental" for short. I call it "mentally composed" because rappers hold the lyrics in their head until they record them, never transferring them to paper or device. You may have heard Jay-Z and those he has mentored proclaim to use this method of composition. There were rumors Jay-Z had borrowed this technique from the Notorious B.I.G., but a 2016 Vlad tv interview with DJ Clark Kent reveals that after a session with Jay-Z, it was in fact the other way around. The Notorious B.I.G. was the one inspired to stop writing lyrics down on paper after seeing Jay-Z do it, reported saying, "He didn't want to be the guy out here writing, when this guy can do that" (that is, compose mentally).

Nowadays, many rappers at least dabble in mental composition. It has become somewhat of a rite of passage to transition from written raps to mental compositions. However, more than just a novelty, this method has some clear advantages. The composition process doesn't get bogged down by the conventions of writing such as correct spelling, legible handwriting, and at a most basic level, keeping a reliable supply of paper and pens (or a charged battery for those that write their raps on a laptop or smartphone). On the other hand, there are some disadvantages. This style really tests your memory. And since it is usually done on the spot, shortly before recording, it can also test the patience of your producer and engineer, if, of course, your name is not Jay-Z.

The mental composition process naturally doesn't lend itself to explanation in writing, but imagine I was with you, speaking in this next passage. You throw on a beat, and this triggers a memory of my last video. I begin rapping:

LOOK AT THE TEXT OF THIS LESSON TO THE EMSEE
A lesson only with your third eye you can see

I may repeat it once or twice until the next line comes to me, then I add:

NOW LOOK AT THE TEXT, THESE ARE LESSONS TO THE

EMSEES

A lesson only with your third eye you can see

I bend speech [pregnant pause]
Bend speech to beats over an MP [Akai MPC drum machine]

In the first lines, notice how "emsee" changes to "emsees" and "look at the text" becomes "Now look at the text, these are lessons to the emsees." As I add more, I'm also improving upon the previous lines. These revisions occur mentally. My last bar, "I bend speech," may not thematically match the beginning lines yet, but this line will change too before I'm ready to record.

As the verse gets longer and longer and approaches the standard sixteen bars, I must begin each recitation with "Now look at the text, these are lessons to the emsees," or whatever else it evolves into. Instead of committing this writing, I keep it all in my head, which is different from simply making it up as I'm going along. Hence, it's unlike freestyle off the top. This is more planned. It is a great mental exercise; it helps you actually "see" words in your mind without the intermediary of pen and paper. Poetry scholar Roland Barthes believed once a poem is committed to paper, the words "die," forever frozen at that point in time. In that sense, mental compositions have more "life," allowing, for example, "emsee" to grow into "emsees."

Composing mentally is therefore not freestyling. You're actually thinking of what plan to say, and you're going to keep building and building by adding more words to it, adding more ideas to it. Eventually, you will have to rap the verse flawlessly. If you are unable to repeat the verse in one take, I strongly suggest you resort to writing it down. Remember, the producer and engineer will already be slightly impatient that you didn't walk into the recording session with composed lyrics, especially if the session isn't booked with composition in mind—composing in a session can be costly, if you are paying for it). You may damage your relationship with the production team by trying to figure out music that most people assume would be ready before the session. Constant fixes and adjustments, such as multiple takes (recording the same verse several times, then deciding which version is the best) or "punch-ins" (rewinding the vocal recording to a few seconds before the mistake, then in a move akin to Double Dutch, finding the perfect space to jump into the recording) take up enough time on their own.

OFF THE TOP

Empty your mind, be formless, shapeless—like water. Now you put water in a cup, it becomes the cup; you put water into a bottle, it becomes the bottle; you put it in a teapot, it becomes the teapot. Now, water can flow, or it can crash. Be water my friend.

I love this Bruce Lee quote because this is the state of freedom needed to operate on the highest level of expression. In expression, there is an intellectual as well as an intuitive approach. Going "off the top" is where the emsee learns to trust his or her intuition and become one with the music, in a way that is immersive and not as much as an external participant.

Before you say a word to the beat, I want you to "empty your mind," like Bruce Lee. In order to go "off the top," the most important thing is that you are no longer distracted. You must learn in this moment to embrace mistakes. In fact, as an emsee, you must know there are NO mistakes, because going off the top is in real-time, it is improvised. There is only "one take," which means no "retakes" nor can there be any mistakes or miss-takes. I want you to become one with your mistakes until they are no longer mistakes. What does this mean? The more you practice your off the top raps (even when they are unintended), the more you'll trust your intuition and doubt yourself less. Trust your intuition and cast away all doubt and fear, and then focus on the beat. For example, let's say you are going off the top and a word comes out in an unintended way, you can acknowledge that it was accidental by saying, "Okay, that wasn't even a word" or "wait, what the heck am I talkin bout? I don't know where that came from, how did that thought come out?" and continue rapping. Even if you make up a word, you can continue effortlessly, if you don't think it was a death blow to your rhyme. The only real mistake is thinking that you can made a mistake.

Rapping "off the top" (of the head) require emsees to see words in their mind's eye and to access them at will. Everywhere you look, words are there. As an emsee, you must see words even when they are not right in front of you.

In coming off the top, the only thing that should matter is the beat and your connection to it. Now, when I say the beat, I want to be very clear: I mean not only the instrumental playing through the speakers or headphones; I also mean the beat or rhythm always playing in your mind's eye (or third ear, if you will). As an emsee, you are learning to see the unseen and hear the unheard. Listen to the silence and find the rhythm in it.

There are rhythms everywhere. Start with your heartbeat. But if you listen further, you will notice rhythm in the trees when the wind blows, when it rains, in the windshield wipers, and as people walk. I see people walking and I hear 2/4 and 4/4 time signatures. I even hear rhythm in blinking lights. My brain assigns rhythms to any consistent motion that's in front of me. And it is finding this rhythm, embracing this rhythm, that is so crucial to off the top raps.

According to the legends of Hip Hop, and in contrast to prevailing opinions, "freestyling" is not coming "off the top" of the head. The legends who invented the term "freestyling" meant something different. The originators of freestyling meant that you had to do something with any random verse you had laying around or something that you wanted people to hear. Freestyling was a way to show off your skill and that was it.

"Off the top," however, is something different. Off the top is a method of improvisation in the form of rap. You are probably most familiar with "battle rap," where two emcees compete in a contest of creating spontaneous raps, often involving a humorous or unflattering reference to the other emcee (known as a "diss"). Such battles in the beginning of Hip Hop were often off the top of the head, created in real time. Incorporating any preplanned rhymes was considered cheating to some purist, though

Hip Hop has evolved from that position. Some classic battles involved large amounts in prize money, and the organizers would often go through extreme measures to ensure artist were "comin' off the top." This might include not allowing competitors to see each other prior to performance (so no one can begin planning rhymes about another emcee's appearance), tossing out random words throughout the competition that must be immediately incorporated in the rhyme, or disallowing common rap clichés (such as comparing your rival to the most recent losing side of a sports championship or proclaiming your rival's significant other would prefer to be with you).

Off the top is also an art form within itself. A few artists such as Supernatural, Juice, King Los, Juice WRLD, as well as myself have tried to continue the long-standing tradition of going "off the top" and I don't see it going anywhere anytime soon. An entire song that mirrors a traditional rap song in format could in fact be spontaneous. You could come off the top with the chorus or the hook. You could come off the top with the verse. Off the top just means we're making it up as we're going along. You say whatever comes to your mind; you're almost saying it without thinking. This can often result in simple nonsense bars, but poetically clever phrasings. I once said in a freestyle battle, "You're like Santa Claus with no beard, you look weird." Why did that come to me? I haven't the slightest clue! But it earned laughs and applause from the audience.

I have had to develop terms for approaches to off the top, which I've divided into formatted and unformatted approaches. Until now, these concepts hadn't been named. Since Hip Hop strongly values self-reliance and frowns upon mentorship, there were no terms for most maneuvers in rap. Many scholars have clumsily attempted to graft poetry terms onto Hip Hop. However, I think it's important that we inside Hip Hop write our own history. I therefore came up with terms that made sense as a Hip-Hop artist and because it is important to approach going off the top with your full vision as an emsee.

In coming off the top, we could start with the first word that comes to mind. I may step into a studio or on stage, and my eyes immediately gravitates to the Bass Guitar and I'm like,

Okay, Bass Guitar
Y'all know I'm about to take this far

I could take that word and then form the rhyme around it. I consider this approach an *unformatted off the top*: rhyming without any attention to measure or theme. There is another method that I call *formatted off the top*. A formatted off the top, while still unplanned, does follow conventional measure and is thematic. And so, if you gave me the words "bass guitar," instead of saying the words "bass guitar" immediately, I would think of the words I hear and then quickly gather my thoughts on that topic. This *is* a form of mental composition, but it's not the same. There is no time taken to build the rhyme; you are doing this in real time, and yet it is still spontaneous. The only difference is that you understand the power of the mind, and you use this power to accomplish multiple tasks at once.

So, when prompted by "bass guitar," this time I might say,

Amazing one
On the bass guitar like James Jamerson

Or

As a musician I got somethin' to bring
On the keys on the drums or pluckin' the strings

In this version, I constructed a complete thought, focusing on the meaning of the words "bass guitar," not just its sound or assonance. The *unformatted* is whatever thought comes to you first. You just say it, and then you create the rhyme afterward. Its strength comes from the complexity of the rhyme scheme or its sheer breadth. Rhyming "guitar" with "far," as in the first example, may not seem impressive, if you simply see it as rhyming "far" with "guitar," but it is a lot more complicated when you have a knowledge of syllable rhyming.

The concept of the unformatted is about guiding your mind and shaping your thoughts. You could constantly add, for instance, to that example by saying:

Okay, BASS GUITAR
Y'all know I'm about to TAKE THIS FAR.
No matter where I am I am a MAJOR STAR *when I'm**
CRE*ATING BARS...*

And on and on. None of these lines are the most complicated bars; some aren't directly related to a bass guitar. However, hearing them live, knowing the rhymes were created in real time, earns an audience's appreciation for the sheer volume. After the tenth or twelfth bar, fans start to smile and gasp. I imagine them thinking, "how many words can he [or she] possibly rhyme with 'guitar' without stopping to think about it?"

In the *formatted freestyle*, its uniqueness comes from the ability to stay on theme. Skeptical fans are quick to call out off the top rhymes that tend to drift off topic. For example, if I followed the above *formatted off the top* with,

> *Keyboards and pen-tricks*
> *Bass-lines sounding like Hendrix*

Astute listeners would groan, "Jimi Hendrix wasn't known for playing a *bass* guitar!" This would be an excusable mistake where the rhyme scheme was more complex, but it would still definitely stand out. Sticking with simplistic mono-syllabic rhymes, however, should allow for more brain power to devote to the theme, and thus accurately recall famous bassists without skipping a beat. In this sense, formatted off the top is more difficult.

I spent some time studying neuroscience when I was teaching *The Art of Rap* at Temple University. Science supports the gut feeling that comin' off the top isn't easy. I'll save a deep dive into the science for later, but there is a process through which we juggle thoughts held in the various parts of the brain. Before speaking any sentence, those words have traveled through many parts of the brain. These different parts must recognize a stimulus, realize how to respond, find the words associated with that response, think of these words in the mind, and then tell your mouth to speak these words (for those of us who are bilingual, there's also the in-between step of translating these words before speaking them). Comin' off the top requires that these processes speed up and overlap.

The good news is that this process is teachable. First, you must relax. The music is happening. Don't rush to say a line, just relax. Be prepared for the moment when the thought and topic come to you. You can practice this at home. Practice looking around the room for items with multiple uses or even the things that may not seem interesting. Put on a beat, look around the room, and study the characteristics of the things around you. Which objects grab your attention? List in your mind the details of each thing you see. Give each object a fair review. Sometimes, the most boring object could have an interesting backstory. Perhaps you see a pen and you are tempted to skip to the next object but pause for a moment. Think of all the possible scenarios. A pen can be used to sign checks, or occasionally it can be used to draw some art. Or, maybe, you found this pen among objects of a family member who passed away, and even though it no longer works, you can't bring yourself to toss it out.

In my case, I'm in a studio with keyboards behind me. Looking at this keyboard, I must ask myself, if I was going to create an instant off the top verse about it, what are its characteristics? What do I see? No, not just what is in front of me, but what are the many things this item tells me? What are the many stories I can create, thinking about this item?

Staying with the keyboard, there's a modulation wheel, there is a pitch bend, there are black and white keys. That's probably what I first notice. Now, if I think of a verse off the top of my head...

I see
what my eye sees
The very unlikely
opposites attract like black and white keys

The verse is not as complicated as I could have made it but notice that I found a way to add the black and white keys. Before I could do that, I had to think of something that would work thematically. This is also a multi-syllable rhyme, increasing the level of difficulty.

Regardless of the subject matter, you must be a step ahead. From the moment you notice the stove, you must simultaneously think of the pot, the kettle and today's breakfast, then create a rhyme with these concepts. Once you notice the sofa, you also notice the pillows and the throw blanket. Imagine your family on that sofa watching a movie. This rhyme will be centered around these concepts. A true understanding of formatting off the top means you're always thinking ahead of the actual rhyme. So, once more, practice looking around. Go outside and get used to seeing everything as poetry. Everything has words, sometimes literally, such as street signs or billboards. Other things just have words that represent them, such as the names of specific flowers, historic neighborhoods, or people. Think of everything as a potential rhyme. Think of everything as poetry.

I've tried to describe the differences between various types of composition. However, the elements of each can also be combined. A rap may contain some lines that were written, some that were mentally composed, and others that were off the top. The beauty of artistry is that you can create from any direction. So, while you may know the rules, don't get locked into them. These guidelines are used to ultimately prepare you for your own artistry. I call this combination the *extemporaneous*: a rap that includes some lines that were written and some that were not. Perhaps you jotted down a word or two per line, and the rest is off the top. Another artist might write the whole song, then put it away, replacing lines she or he cannot remember with off the top or making a spontaneous decision to replace a line while recording. These are skills you will develop yourself as an artist. That's what makes art so special and so great.

That we have reviewed various forms of composing a rap song, let's look closer at the actual bars. The most basic element of any two lines of rap is the rhyme. At its core, a rhyme is two words that end with the same or similar sounding syllables. However, in rap, the term "rhyme" takes on a slightly different meaning. A rhyme in rap uses not only these two end-line syllables, but sometimes the entire line. So, when I refer to a "rhyme," keep in mind I'm referring not only to the part that rhymes. Indeed, one of the elemental forms of rap where rhyme takes on different meanings is in the art of storytelling.

STORYTELLING

STORYTELLING IN RAP is one of the essential elements. As an

emsee you will become *one* with your imagination. There is an art to storytelling and it is as much a part of the tradition of rap as drums and rhythm, dating back to the *jeliw* or griots in West Africa to Pigmeat Markham's "Here Comes the Judge" and the Jubalaires' "The Preacher and the Bear" in the early 1900s. You will want to revisit this specific topic—and of course others in this section of the book—because it will help you execute story-telling more effectively.

On my song "In and out," I used two words to tell a story of an "*In*dian" dude who lacked humility. The story goes like this:

I was IN and OUT of work when I met my INfluence
He was OUTstanding when playing an INstrument
An INdian dude, very OUTspoken
Had a lot of INput, his OUTlook was kosher
An OUTsider, cats called him dumb,
Men from the hood
Knew he ain't have no INcome
You could tell from his OUTfit he was IN debt
But his INterest wasn't OUTlandish begets
He wasn't INcapable of getting a job yet
He said he was using poverty for an OUTlet
I was INclined to ask with hopes he'd OUTpour
More INsight for just sleeping OUTdoors
Dude told me he had so much pride
When he played his INstrument he tried to OUTshine
His INstructor and became an OUTcast
They INsisted this kid go OUT and

Take his INgenious OUT IN *the open*
So next time he won't be so OUTspoken
I was INtrigued, OUTraged *and I was open*
This INdividual *was an* OUTlaw *and hopeless*
INconceivable *skill,* OUTright *great*
But the pride he had INside *far* OUTweighed
For this reason, he was cast OUTside
Now that's what you get when you INdocile
The moral is don't let pride IN *your house*
Be about bringing truth IN *and I'm* OUT

The track "The Subway" from my self-titled LP also tell stories based on observing people on a train and imagining what their lives were like before and after they left the train. Storytelling has no real formula but there are some reoccurring elements in great storytelling. These elements are setting, characters, protagonist, antagonist, plot, and conflict.

If we use the "In and Out" song as an example, the setting would be the workplace, since I said, "I was in and out of work." The characters are of course the Indian dude, the cats (people) who called him a bum, the men from the hood, the Indian dude's instructor, and me. In this case, the protagonist is the "Indian dude," who clearly is the subject of the story. The antagonists are the "cats (people)" who called him a bum, and the "men from the hood." They are in the story to create some difficulty for the Indian dude. The plot is that this Indian dude was seemingly homeless or poor, but it turns out he was just going through a process of learning humility, taught by his instructor. In the end, the conflict was between the people who thought the Indian dude was just a bum.

All good storytelling has these elements. If you look at some of the best story songs in Hip Hop history, you will find that they all have these elements in common. Though some of them may not have all these elements, you will find them. Eminem's "Stan" is a great example. The story is about an obsessed fan who ends up taking his own life and the life of his pregnant girlfriend because he hadn't received a reply to his many letters sent to Eminem, for whom he claims to be the biggest fan.

This story is a tragedy. But the setting is in this obsessed fan's world and mind through letters he had written. The characters are Stan, his pregnant girlfriend, Stan's little brother, Matthew, and Eminem, who ends up reading one of the letters sent by Stan. The protagonist in this story is Stan, as the entire story is centered around him. The antagonist unknowingly is Eminem himself. The plot is based around how far an obsessed fan can go and the conflict, in this case, is Eminem's fame and his inability to reach *all* the fans who really admire and love his work.

One of the influencers of all modern rap storytelling is Slick Rick the Ruler. The man literally has an album called *The Great Adventures of Slick Rick* and another called *The Art of Storytelling*. Let's examine his classic song, "Children's story." The lyrics begin this way:

Here we go
Once upon a time not long ago
When people wore pajamas and lived life slow

When laws were stern and justice stood
And people were behavin' like they ought ta good
There lived a lil' boy who was misled
By anotha lil' boy and this is what he said
"Me, Ya, Ty, we gonna make sum cash
Robbin' old folks and makin' tha dash"
They did the job, money came with ease
But one couldn't stop, it's like he had a disease
He robbed another and another and a sista and her brotha
Tried to rob a man who was a D.T. undercover
The cop grabbed his arm, he started acting erratic
He said "Keep still, boy, no need for static"

In this story, the setting is "Once upon a time, not long ago when people wore pajamas and lived life slow / When laws were stern and justice stood and people were behaving like they oughta good." Looking back, Slick Rick describes a simpler place and time when he wrote this rhyme. The "once upon a time" phrase has been used in storytelling for ages. He is descriptive of the characters who, as he put it, "the people who wore pajamas." He goes on to write about the protagonist boy, who was misled, the "other lil boy" who was clearly a bad influence and ultimately a stumbling block, those who were robbed including the antagonist, in this case the DT undercover and cops. The plot is about a teenager who is misguided into a life of crime and whose life ends tragically, with the conflict set between the local police and the lead character who chose a life of crime.

Storytelling can be as creative as you would like for it to be.

Remember, you must *see* the story. Imagine details of the place where things are happening. If need be, go to places that are similar, in your imagination, to those you want to write about.

When I am writing stories, I go so far as to imagine the smell of the venue where I'll be in the story, or where the characters are. It is also a good idea to watch plenty of films, specifically drama and thrillers. Although I love almost every genre of film, I am really a fan of films with plot twists for these help by modeling great storytelling as well as the use of wit.

WIT

Rule: Learn the art of humor and verbal intelligence. Learn how to play on words, see words inside of words, emphasize and deemphasize words (the art of the slur), and manipulate words

PLAYING WITH AND on words as marks of verbal intelligence is indispensable to the emsee. In this chapter, we'll learn how to use similes, homonyms, paraphrasing, double entendre, personification, and wordplay.

New Orleans emsee 3'D Natee says:

Every year when I don't get an award it's such a sad reminder
That I get Robbed like Blac Chyna
With no ghostwriter... shout out to Drake though
I ball out like OG Maco

3'D Natee is displaying verbal intelligence or wit. The reference to celebrity Blac Chyna "getting Robbed" is a clever play on words referencing the celebrity's well publicized relationship with Rob (get it!) Kardashian. As clever as that was, let's pay attention to the later part of the bar where she says,

> *shout out to Drake though*
> *I ball out like OG Maco*

This last line about OG Maco is a reference to an unfortunate car accident that left the rapper with one eye. Dope line, even though it came out of something tragic. Thankfully, OG Maco survived and was able to say he liked the line, which shows he has a good sense of humor.

Phonte from Little Brother once rapped, "On some teleprompter sh#t I got you watching your words." This line makes you think of a person reading a teleprompter, which allows the speaker to read words while looking at the camera in order to make reading a speech look natural. So, when Phonte says, "I got you watching your words," it's a clever way of describing how much he has you being careful with what you say to him. This is what "wit" is all about.

SIMILES

WHEN PEOPLE MOST often talk about punchlines, they're really talking about similes. Similes involve the use of "like" or "as" to compare the familiar with the unfamiliar. This helps your listener better understand the unfamiliar. Most commonly in rap, the unfamiliar is the artist him or herself and their lyrical skill. Simple examples include "I shine like the sun" or "Flow like water." Others are more specific, such as "Skills like Monk on the keys," requiring the intended lister to be familiar with jazz pianist Thelonious Monk. Recently, similes evolved into "Hashtag Rap," a style popularized by Big Sean. Other notable rappers to have used this style are Drake and Nicki Minaj. Here, the terms "like" or "as" are implied, and the familiar part of the comparison is treated like a social media hashtag. Such a rhyme might be,

This is rap rock-n-roll #Hendrix
I'm retro with the flow #vintage

Normally, we would simply put "like" in front of "Hendrix" and "vintage," but what makes this concept different is the replacement of "like." Let's try it again,

The style leave all in awe #magic
make em all draw to me #Magnet

HOMONYMS

ANOTHER WAY TO create punchlines is to study words that sound the same but have different meanings. These are called homonyms. Homonyms can help you construct some pretty dope punchlines once you understand the formula. For example, let's take the word "pupil." In a song I wrote called "Zebruh," I used this word with more than one meaning. I said,

Switchin' up the style in unusual
I can see you wanna be my pupil

There is the "I can see" line that plays on the *eye* used to *see*, which could have easily also read, "eye can see you wanna be my pupil." But here, the word *pupil* is being used in two ways. First, I am saying, "I can see you wanna be my pupil (student)," while also saying, "I can see you wanna be my pupil," which points to the *eye* can *see* portion of that lyric.

PARAPHRASING

MASTERING THE USE of similes and homonyms leads into another related part of punchlines: paraphrasing. For instance, J Cole says:

What's the price for a black man life?
I check the toe tag, not one zero in sight
I turn the TV on, not one hero in sight
Unless he dribble or he fiddle with mics

J Cole demonstrates something that the greats do almost without thinking. He is *paraphrasing*. This is another way of being a poetic emsee. Paraphrasing is usually defined as "the act or process of restating or rewording." But how can an emsee "restate" or "reword" something that hasn't been "stated" or "spoken?" Well, remember, you are an emsee. You are learning to hear what hasn't been said and to see what isn't in front of your natural eyes. These words already exist.

First, you must think about what you are going to say. Then, you will think of another way of saying it. Because you have said this in your mind, it is as real as if you had said it to a friend, so you are restating or rewording. Here's another example. Sean Price says: "I smack planes off of buildings, I'm a f#k ape." He is paraphrasing by saying he is "King Kong" without saying the obvious. Yes, saying you are King Kong is a statement of how powerful you are, but that is too easy to create as an emsee. This is where paraphrasing comes into play. Also consider when Chance the Rapper says:

> *Back when I could trust in my dogs like Balto*
> *My family The* SOPRANOS *these n###s is* ALTOS

This is a creative way of saying my squad is tough by likening them to the Mob family from The Sopranos and the others are not as tough. Or, it could also mean that he sees his family elevated above others as a Soprano sings a pitch higher than an alto.

Another example comes from Royce Da 5'9" in the song, "Count for Nothing." He raps:

> *I spit fire like Izod*
> *why not?*
> *Cause sho nuff I'm glowing like Taimak*

In this paraphrasing example, the line "cause sho nuff I'm glowing like Taimak" is a reference to Taimak, who was the lead character from the 1985 martial arts comedy film, *The Last Dragon*. Having the "glow" was a theme in the film. For Taimak's character Leroy Green, aka Bruce Leroy, "having the glow" meant he achieved mastery in the martial arts. Royce could have simply said "I'm glowing like Bruce Leroy" or the Last Dragon, but either phrasing doesn't display wit. What demonstrates wit through paraphrasing is saying the thing that connects us indirectly to what the emsee wants to express.

Let's try paraphrasing a few things so you can get this concept. Let's say you wanted to rap, "I am the new *Thelonious*," referencing the jazz music genius. That is too obvious to say. So, you would think of something not as obvious, a little more indirect. You could then say, "The new creator of the Brilliant corners." If you know the work of Thelonious Monk, you know that he created the album *Brilliant Corners*. This way, you indirectly say you are the new Monk. In another example, you want to say, "I started crying." You could say that, or you could say, instead, "My eyes flooded." This is more poetic. Remember, rhythm and poetry, since the goal is always to be as poetic as possible.

THE DOUBLE ENTENDRE

THE TRADITIONAL INTERPRETATION of a double entendre is a word or phrase open to two interpretations, with one of the meanings being risqué or indecent. But that is not the only way it is used in rap. A line from my *Rapsloitation* LP says, "If you don't like this disc get Qtip's." I am using a double meaning: one, the rapper Qtip, the other a cotton swab used to clean out the ears. The Notorious B.I.G.'s lyric, "If Faith had twins they would have been 2Pac's," is another example of a double entendre. Twins mean two babies, implying that they would belong to rapper Tupac Shakur aka 2Pac.

The way to pull this technique off is to find homonyms and leave them open to interpretation. As an emsee, you must learn to see rap from a higher vantage point and to be okay with the meaning of your lyrics not always being obvious. This is high-level communication. That said, let's try this exercise. Let's take the word *buy*, which, when spoken, has multiple meanings and can be interpreted in different ways. If I were to turn this word into a double entendre, I could say,

I left the store with a great deal and good BYE

This could mean I left the store and wished the store manager or someone in the store well, or it could be a reference to the fact that I made a "good buy," that I got a great deal.

Let's look at another word with more than one meaning, *died*. I could say, "The man's hair turned grey and then he *died*." This could mean the man's hair turned grey and then he passed away of old age, or it could also mean, he decided to *dye* his hair. These are some examples of double entendre and how to use them. Think of words that have more than one meaning and think of two or more scenarios where you can use them. The goal is to be as vague as possible, so that you don't steer the listener towards a specific meaning.

PERSONIFICATION

PERSONIFICATION IS ABOUT imagining one thing as another, using the art of reinterpretation. Personification occurs when you give nature or human characteristics to something nonhuman, or an abstract quality in human form. One of the best examples in Hip Hop is Common's "I Used to Love H.E.R." Here Hip Hop itself is described as if it were an actual person, specifically an ex-girlfriend. The use of *personification* emphasizes how much Common loves Hip Hop music and how disappointed he was by its commercialization.

Creating personification takes thought; you will have to apply the attributes of one thing to another. For example, Nas's "I Gave you Power" and Tupac Shakur's "Me and My Girlfriend" both talk about a gun as a person. Nas raps from the perspective of the gun while 2 Pac raps from the perspective of a person in a relationship with a gun. An exercise for personification involves looking at objects and trying to humanize them. For example, if a brush were human, what would it feel? How would it think and what would a conversation with this brush sound like?

This is how you can learn to create personification in your raps. The process requires an obvious subject, and a not so obvious subject. If I am going to rap about a city, for example, I could use the city of Philadelphia. I would need to think about presenting the obvious subject, so you won't know I am talking about Philadelphia. In order to do this effectively, you are going to think of similarities between the obvious subject and Philadelphia. If I do the obvious comparison, where I rap about Philadelphia as a woman I am in love with, then I'll say something that's vague:

When we first met you were kind of cold to me

At first glance, the line could mean this woman I'm describing wasn't very nice to me when we first met. But, in the context of personification, this could also be a reference to the weather in Philadelphia, which gets very cold during the winter.

Think creatively about things that could be personified. Personification is often confused with metaphors because they are similar. Metaphors, however, are used to make your statements sound more poetic, for example, on "Frankincense and Myrrh" Sa Roc says, "I'm Peter Parker superhero to this language arts." Her statement is a *metaphor*. Personification is about seeing things as concepts, and not just what's in front of you. Once again, as an emsee, your objective is to *see*, so keep all your eyes open.

WORDPLAY

WORDPLAY IS ULTIMATELY about seeing words inside of words, the art of dissecting words by syllables. Wordplay is when we flip the sounds and meanings of words, in order to come up with something creative. Typically, the creative use of words will cause the listener to play it again. The original MC, master of ceremonies, had the job of moving the crowd, which eventually moved to recorded music. These recordings brought about *rewind culture*. Someone wanting to rewind your lyrics meant that you said something so dope, they either missed what was said or liked it so much they had to hear it again. Wordplay is no different. In my Premo freestyles, I use this technique, saying,

> *So concerned with the peace and just* TRYNA TALK
> *I'll come back as a tree just to* DIE A LOG

The wordplay here concerns the phrase "die a log," which is a play on words for dialogue. I broke the multi-syllable word "dialogue" into three words. Now, this won't work with every multi-syllable word. You would have to make sure that the word, when dissected into individual syllables, can stand the test.

In another example, Hopsin says,

> *I'm such a* CONTRADICTION, *I hang with Dizzy Wright*
> *And all he does is smoke so when I'm breathing all the*
> GANJA GETS IN
> NOT TO MENTION *I'm* CONDESCENDING, *my* MIND IS
> MISSING
> *Plus I'm* KINDA SENDING *the wrong signal*
> *Oh* GOD, I'M SICKENING

Notice the word "condescending" becomes "kinda sending" or "kind of sending." As you become one with words, you will begin to hear words inside of words as Hopsin did in this example.

Let's practice this. An emsee can create wordplay with the near impossible word. In fact, at times, I like to just throw words out and create some dope wordplay out of what most might think as nothing. The first word that comes to mind is "music." Most would not imagine what wordplay could come out of that two-syllable word. But what I heard is "Muse sick." And so, a dope wordplay line could be, "My songs can make a muse sick 'cos they're so ill." This play on words using "muse" (someone who is a source of inspiration) and "sick," which I linked to "ill" (Hip Hop slang for really good) is an example.

The trick is to find words inside of words. Look specifically for multi-syllable words. So, "dummy" becomes "dumb me." Multi-tasking becomes "multi-task king." Once you learn this principle, which is to see words inside of words, you will be able to do clever wordplay at will. So, practice looking for words inside of words and you will become a master at wordplay, a major part of the art of word manipulation.

WORD MANIPULATION

WHEN MY FELLOW Philadelphian emsee Black Thought from The Roots rhymes:

Obi-Wan universe, you owe me own SOLID
My homie GONZALEZ *only know gun* VIOLENCE
On the corner, where they PROBABLY *on they 21* SAVAGE
Catch two in your CABBAGE *young Cesar* CHAVEZ

He is demonstrating a technique I call WORD MANIPULATION. Word manipulation occurs when you take a word and reinterpret how you pronounce it. The word "solid" doesn't typically rhyme with "savage" and "cabbage" doesn't normally rhyme with "violence." But when you emsee, this is possible. Once more, an emsee must see what is unseen and hear what is unheard.

Let's look at the word "idiot." In his 1998 freestyle, the late great Big L rapped,

I throw slugs at IDIOTS
no love for CITY COPS

Visually, the ending words don't rhyme, but the genius of this phrasing is the very technique of word manipulation. Big L doesn't pronounce "idiots" the normal way; he pronounces it, "i-di-ots." This way, he has taken the word and distorted it. I-DI-OT (pronounced "id-Dee-ahht") makes a perfect rhyme out of a word that originally wouldn't have worked in that specific rhyme scheme.

In one of my older rhymes, I distorted the word "formula." The setup I used went something like this:

I see you rhyme for MULA [slang for money]
but ya'll that's not my FOR-MULA

I was able to make this work phonetically, even musically, by pronouncing the latter part of formula as "mew luh," the word becomes "for-mew-la." Distorting words is not only about making words rhyme that normally wouldn't work, it also helps with the musicality or dexterity of your raps.

Practice word manipulation by saying words aloud, in different ways. For example, try pronouncing the word I just used, "aloud," as "a-lode" or "aye-loud." Or, example as "EGG-ZAM-PO," ignorant as "IG-NO-RENT," or standard as "Stan-daurd" (pronounced like vanguard). This will open an entirely new universe of rhymes, as you will practically never run out of ways to distort words. If you combine all these elements I have taught you, you will have the strategy to rhyme infinitely as an emsee.

ALLITERATION

ALLITERATION IS WHEN you take one consonant sound and repeat it at least three times in succession. A consonant is a speech sound that is not a vowel. It also refers to letters of the alphabet that represent those sounds: Z, B, T, G, and H are all consonants. 2Pac used alliteration in the song "If I Die Tonight," where he rapped, "*P*olish your *p*istols *p*repare for battle *p*ast the *p*ump." He purposely uses "P" consistently to make the rhyme more stylish. For further examples, check out J live's "Mcee" or Blackalicious' "Alphabetic Aerobics," where he rapped, "*g*ift *g*ot *g*reat *g*lobal *g*oods *g*one *g*lorious...."

The easiest way to learn alliteration would be using a dictionary. You should study the dictionary anyway, but in alliteration, this is a big help. You can always go to a specific section and find the words that start with the same consonant and create rhymes around those words.

EPENTHESIS

EPENTHESIS MEANS THE insertion of one or more sounds or letters within a word. A crucial technique to emseeing is the goal of symmetry. Symmetry means creating harmonious and beautiful proportion and balance. In other words, symmetry is making the different bars sound even. To achieve symmetry on the song "The Next Movement," Black Thought of The Roots uses epenthesis when he raps:

> *You doubt the illa-fifth what could you* ACCOMPLISH
> *Whether they skywriting your name or you* ANONYMOUS

By simply adding the "ah" sound in the right place, Black Thought creates a perfect 4 syllable rhyme scheme that balances the phrasing and creates a sound more pleasing to the ear. The word *accomplish* is obviously a 3-syllable word, while *anonymous* has 4 syllables. The problem with matching these bars is that they are uneven or asymmetrical. In order to create lyrical symmetry, Black Thought inserts the "ah" sound and pronounces the word *a-ccom-pah-lish*. By adding the "ah" sound as a 3rd syllable before "lish," Black Thought accomplishes a crucial technique in emseeing.

On the song "Memories Live" from the 2000 *Reflection Eternal* album, Talib Kweli raps:

> *Well I drop it in the pocket*
> *because rocking's my occupation*
> *I do it* REMARKABLY,
> SPARK UP A LEAF

The word *remarkably* contains 4 syllables, as does the phrase "spark up a leaf"—spark (1) up (2) a (3) leaf (4). As Black Thought did, Talib Kweli inserts the "ah" sound and pronounces the word *rem-ar-ka-b*a-lee, which is now a 5-syllable word. In order to create rhyme symmetry, he rhymes the last 4 syllables of the word ARKABLY (or *ar-ka-ba-lee*) with SPARK UP A LEAF. When you use the technique of epenthesis, you can restructure words and open up entirely new worlds of word manipulation. The key is to make sure the words are still recognizable. Too much restructuring and the words may take on entirely different meanings, in which case, you lose the original intent of the lyric.

ELLISON

WORDS ARE MALLEABLE. The ability to hear the most important part of a word and to deemphasize its different parts is yet another skill. We call this Ellison, or when you leave out a sound or syllable when speaking. Ellison could be a "slurring" of your words, but this technique can be valuable in opening a universe of rhyming for the emsee. In the song "Mortal Thought," the Teacha KRS-One says:

> *You're full of more junk than a* SAUSAGE
> *Let me show you what a real Hip Hop* ARTIST IS

He has used the technique known as Ellison. In this case, he condensed the words "artist is," focusing on the phonetic sounds "ar is" (pronounced "AW IZ"). Keep in mind the word sausage is pronounced "saw-sidge," which could be word manipulation or just KRS' New York accent. The main point is that certain aspects of the phrase "artist is" was deemphasized in order to make this rhyme work.

From my *Rapsloitation* LP, I rap:

> *I see the world as* COMICAL *and yet* KINDA BLUE
> *My* OPTIC VIEW *is probably set on* MONO HUE
> *The 2nd coming of* AMARU
> *The* HONORABLE...

I want you to focus on the last two lines: "The 2nd coming of Amaru / the honorable." The word honorable is typically pronounced "AH-NOR-RUBBLE." But using the technique of elision, I deemphasized a portion of that word, specifically the "NOR" part, to get something that sounds more like "AHN-RUBBLE." This makes the rhyme more aesthetically pleasing to the ear even though the word has been altered.

To practice this technique, you must learn to look at words as malleable. When you are writing a verse, as you are forming the words, practice saying them in different ways. Try this with the word "salivate": you can turn it into "sal-vate." The word "sal-vate" in isolation or without context could sound like gibberish, but this would change if I said,

> *I used to rush on the track, but I* NOW WAIT
> *I'm hungry hearing the beat, I straight* SAL-VATE

Adding the phrase, "I'm hungry hearing the beat," creates the context for the listener so that when the deliberately mispronounced word is said, it registers as "salivate."

ADVANCED RHYMING

ADVANCED RHYMING IS the science of the vowel and the art of verbal math, and this begins with mastering multi-syllabic rhymes (rhyming more than one syllable in a verse) and assonance. Let's start with multi-syllabic rhymes.

When Masta Ace says, "Welcome to the *rap crucifixion* /Every other day it's like a *brand new conviction*," or when Big Pun says, "You know the *Pun'll diss you* / if your whole steez is *unofficial*," both exhibit the art of multi-syllable rhyming.

Rhyming more than one syllable in rhyme schemes, multi-syllable rhymes allow you to sit down and analyze words in almost a mathematical way. It's fun and at times can be therapeutic. To demonstrate how this works, let's think of a word like "music." Now, replace this word with the phonetic sounds you hear. Instead of "music," hear it as "Ooh-ihh." To better rhyme a word, you must ignore the word itself. When you hear it that way, it opens you up to a universe of words and sounds that could work. Restricted to the traditional method, "music" might be a difficult word to rhyme. However, thinking in terms of sound instead of letters, "music" could then rhyme with:

Use it
lose it

blue is
Foolish
tune in
do it
ruined

From my song "Hocus Pocus," I rap:

Pay attention 'cause I AIN'T REPEATING MYSELF
Some of you spit on a track, I AM RELIEVING MYSELF
Out OF THE EAST ILLADELPH
SOLDIER THAT'S BLOWING OPEN THE CULTURE
The CULPRIT OF KILLING VULTURES, EXPOSE IT AND
TAKE IT OVER

Notice, in "I ain't repeating myself," "*I ain't*" rhymes with the second line ("*I am*" phonetically), and "repeating" and "relieving" both have three syllables. You can constantly use that. Always try and focus on the most prominent sounds in the word to create the rhyme. For example, you can take a word like "animal" and break it into three syllables, where animal becomes "a-ni-mal." So now, you can get:

I RAPPED-THESE-FLOWS
AND SUR-PASS-THESE-FOLKS,
A BEAST ON THE MIC CALL ME A-NI-MAL

In one of my favorite Lauryn Hill verses from the song "Mystery of Iniquity," she says,

...Polluted, recruited and suited judicial charm
And the defense, isn't making any sense?
Faking the confidence of escaping the consequence
That a defendant is depending on the system...

Notice the phrasing, "*Faking the confidence of escaping the conse-quence.*" Lauryn is rhyming "Faking the consequence / and *scaping the consequence.*" The rhyme scheme doesn't include the "of" in these lyrics, or the "e" (pronounced "EH" from the word "escap-ing"). This is high-level, multi-syllable rhyming, six syllables to be precise. This is also an example of why L Boogie is considered one of the elite lyricists.

When you create multi-syllable rhymes, you're breaking down multi-syllable words, syllable by syllable. This form of musical math can be measured and delivered on the mic. Of the many things one can do with rap, this is mentally fun, because you start hearing words differently once you fully embrace this method. In fact, after a while, you will not be able to hear multi-syllable words the same again.

At this point, you are hearing the phonetic sounds of a word more than anything. Throughout my work, I use multi-syllable rhymes all the time. In the Ntro to my *A Lack of Convention*, I say:

you're welcome to debate
whether he changed the LANDSCAPE
with a lack of convention. Every record the MAN MAKES

I divided landscape into two words and rhymed each word separately, and thus "landscape" with "man makes." Instead of hearing the details of the word, I am focusing on the phonetic sounds of the word, which means I'm hearing "*landscape man makes.*" Here are the lines again:

> *you're welcome to debate*
> *whether he changed the* LANDSCAPE
> *with a lack of convention. Every record the* MAN MAKES

The wordsmith Elzhi, formerly of Slum Village, has brilliant symmetry in his multi-syllable writing. Here's an example:

> *You know many times that there was* RENT DUE
> *and I ain't have a* CENT TO,
> *my name, is that the same* STENT YOU WENT THROUGH?

Or, in "Brag Swag," where he says,

> *Have you rest, above the crest moon*
> *On* YOUR BLOCK, *get your* DOOR KNOCKED
> *Then by my* WARLOCKS, *who* WORE GLOCKS *And left you*
> *with stains too deep for* CLOROX

Notice the breakdown of the words, "warlocks" and "Clorox." They are broken down by syllable to create two-syllable rhyme patterns.

In "My Life," the legend Kool G Rap put a four-syllable rhyme scheme together:

COPPED THE LATEST EVERY HOT FLAVOR IN THEM
CROCS AND GATORS
Somebody clique riff, POP THE BRAVEST
Out of town trips in whips I GOT FROM AVIS, drop
KNOTS IN VEGAS
My PLOT FOR PAPER was CROCKPOTS OF WAFERS

Let's count the syllables: copped (1) the (2) la- (3) test (4) / Crocs (1) and (2) ga- (3) tors (4). Note that "tors" in ga*tors* is pronounced like "is" NOT "or," and so the pronunciation is "gay-tis" instead of "gay-tors" for rhyme effect.

Kool G Rap illustrates one of the advanced tricks of being an emsee, understanding the art of hearing words as sounds, or hearing them phonetically. Instead of hearing the exact words with all their details, you must let the details of the words go. They are not the priority right now. And this way, you can form rhyme schemes more easily. Words are flexible—they can bend—and so the more rigid you are, the less you'll be able to do with them.

If you've ever been in a studio with a person writing raps, initially these raps are often utterances to the rhythm. In this part of the creative process, the individual is simply mumbling words. Ultimately, we want to match actual words to these utterances. Simply put, we are looking for similar sounding words to match the sounds we mumbled. This is where a lot of emsees start. There is an entire genre of mumbling and slurring words that many enjoy, which may have originated in the creative stages, or the art of emseeing, but that's another topic for another time. Let's move on to assonance.

ASSONANCE

ASSONANCE IS THE repetition of a vowel sound. The power of
the vowel in rhyming can't be understated, precisely because the
vowel sound is the most important part of a word in rhyming.
Assonance is also a poetic element often used in rap. Through assonance, we are introduced to an entire universe for rhyming. Assonance takes on importance because rap uses slang, and slang
usually means not necessarily pronouncing words with detailed
enunciation. Of course, enunciation is important, and it has its
place. But the beauty of rap is that we are not bound by enunciation. So, we could take a word like "groove" and use it in the following rhyme:

> *So listen to the groove*
> *to the pitch and to the mood As I hit you with a tune*
> *something different this is new*

Too much focus on the beginning or ending constant sound prevents us from rhyming "groove" and "tune." But here, we're not
overemphasizing the consonant sounds. Instead, we're stressing
the "oooh" sound. Here's another example:

> *Definition of sm*oo*th*
> *They look, they like, D*u*de*
> *Too dope and too c*oo*l.*
> *How I make the bars gr*oo*ve*

Notice how the "*oooh*" sound stands out again. Though this

sound is in the middle of each final word, the rhyme works when pronounced in a way that doesn't emphasize the ending consonant. Keep in mind, however, these ending consonant sounds must be close enough for the deemphasis to go unnoticed. You could, for example, rhyme "hand" with "slam." However, "hand" and "cat" would be trickier, though that could work by distorting either word.

There are many who are great at this technique, but there is one artist I would highlight in this regard, Canibus. As an emsee, he has proven to be one of the greats over the years, and in relation to this specific technique (along with many others), he has also proven to be a master of this style. In "Bop ya Head" by Killer Priest, Canibus raps:

> ...*the pain'll make your voice change* OCTAVES
> *from low pitch to* HIGH PITCH

Notice how the word "octaves" does not visually rhyme with "high pitch," but phonetically he is able to make this work. When you learn to hear words as sounds, this opens an entire universe of rhymes and rhyme schemes. Once your rhymes are written, they of course must then be said aloud, which is an art form within itself.

VOING

Rule: Learn the art of the voice and how to breathe. Rapping is not only about what you say, but how you say it. Master the art of vocal inflections, the rise and fall of pitch and the essentials of vocal presentation

T HE ART OF breathing is central to mastering the voice, its inflections, pitch and cadence. But there are two kinds of voices. We all have an *inner voice* and an *outer voice*. The inner voice is the true voice, the voice that is closest to our real thoughts and desires. The outer voice is the voice we project into the world. This voice represents us and is our spokesperson. The inner voice is your companion and its development have immense benefits. Listening to this voice can help in times of doubt and despair, and can calm the storm in your mind. A vital goal of the emsee is to synchronize your inner and outer voices, so that the confidence that you think will be projected. Ultimately, these aspects of voice is what leads to great delivery, on stage or in the recording studio.

BREATH CONTROL

IN THE ERA of recording, the art of breathing can seem dated. It's easy to assume technology has all but replaced breath control. Perhaps you are familiar with the studio jargon "overdubs," "edits," "punch-ins," or even "adlibs." In overdubs, a rapper will say a word, line, or sometimes a whole verse two or more times. A mistake in pronunciation or cadence is masked by layering the multiple takes. Edits consist of erasing the parts that contain the mistake and replacing it with a new recording of a word or line. Finally, punch-ins are frequently used in modern recording in "double time" raps (rap songs with three syllables per note). Where or when an artist stops or stutters, they then pick it up a line or two before the mistake, and the engineer begins the recording once the artist re-syncs with the original recording. This method is less perceptible to the average listener. If done flawlessly, a rapper that lacks the ability to rap double time live in concert can create the illusion of double-time breath control.

Knowing how and when to breathe can open great stylistic possibilities. And it is important for the true lyricist and emcee to understand this concept so that their live performances can be as great as in-studio performances. In the song "This is Genius Level Hip Hop," I say,

Now I'm in the middle of a lot of mediocrity
And everybody claiming that they gotta be
A hot emcee to tell me

And now they wanna tell me all you gotta do is ride the beat,
It's all about the rhythm man I'm tellin' you it's gotta be...

When you read, or listen in your mind, to the recording closely, you'll notice that I take a breath before the phrase, "Now I'm in the middle...." The breaths in rap are almost like sips of air because you don't have time for a full breath. This requires practice. You don't want it to be too obvious. Almost no respected recording, including those of live concerts, contains audible draws of breath.

It is therefore important to work on strengthening your lungs. There are many exercises that can help. By holding your breath and counting to a number in your head, you can push your capacity to hold your breath. I have battled asthma (a disease that affects the lungs) since the beginning of my career and have had to learn to work around it.

As a method of practice, you can use the example of "Genius Level Hip Hop" and say it along with me. Try not to fumble the words and to be as articulate as I am in the recording. You can also try rapping while walking, or even jogging. Anything that will help with breathing and improving the strength of your lungs will be useful.

Controlling your breath can be the difference in a good delivery and a bad one. I find that mint tea is great. It helps my breathing, because peppermint contains menthol, which improves airflow in the nasal cavity and can make breathing easier. You need to know that controlling your breath is all about the art of exhalation. Yes, there is inhalation, but that is the least challenging part. The key is how fast you exhale, because this will determine how much power you'll have when delivering your verse.

The more words you are trying to deliver, the more conservative you will need to be when exhaling. Remember, words are your notes on an instrument, and you are the instrument. If you think about it, especially as an emsee, you are a percussive wind instrument. Percussive because you are closer to the drum than you are to the violin in terms of pitch.

CADENCE AND PITCH

LEARNING HOW TO make the pitch of your voice rise and fall give words and sentences different meanings as well as emphasizes certain points. This is the art of pitch, also known as cadence. On the 1996 song "Woo Hah," Busta Rhymes says,

Busta rhymes up in the PLACE true in-deed

Notice the emphasis on *place*. This is a clever use of cadence. Though Busta's longevity is because of a complete mastery of all the elements, including *cadence and pitch*, there is one thing that is consistent with this genius—his understanding of his voice and how to use it.

Cadence is the rise and fall of your voice when you're rapping. Usually, the most important word of any sentence is emphasized by saying it slightly *louder* than the rest of the words in that sentence. Read the following rhyme with emphasis on the capitalized words:

Listen to the RHYME *that I'm spitting*
Off the top of the MIND *when I'm ripping*

Here, I want to emphasize that this rap is a freestyle, so I stress "rhyme" and "mind." I say these words at a different volume. It can even change the meaning. If I were to say, "My style is *my own,*" with emphasis on the phrase "my own," I'm most likely responding to an accusation of copying someone else's style. However, if I say, "*My* style is my own," with emphasis on the first "my," it now sounds as if I'm making accusations that another rapper is copying me.

The greats weren't afraid to use *different* tones. When you listen closely to 2Pac, he did a lot of "Let all my *enemies,*" which would often be expressed as "en-e-meeeease," stressing the "ease" portion by raising his voice at that point. That creates vocal excitement. *Tones* bring life and character to words.

Although his name speaks to his remarkable technique, emsee Tech N9ne is a master at changing his cadence when he raps. His style skillfully combines rhythm, cadence, and pitch, and he can change his vocal tone at will. Now, these skills are made to seem effortless, but extremely talented emcees like Tech N9ne, Chubb Rock and U.K. emsee Lady Leshurr have had to work on executing them. Check out Lady Leshurr's "Your Mr," Tech N9ne's "Strangeulation vol II Cypher 1," and Chubb Rock's "The Mind 1997."

We use tones in everyday storytelling. Read the following narrative in a monotone (straight tone) voice, and concentrate on keeping your voice at the same volume:

I happened to go outside when I saw the police, and they were arresting this guy. They placed him in handcuffs and threw him in the back of the squad car. Meanwhile, a woman was crying, "please don't take my baby."

The excitement is not there. It's difficult to tell what is remarkable or novel about this story. Now, try it again, but emphasize the capitalized words:

I happened to go OUTSIDE when I saw the POLICE, and they were ARRESTING this guy. They placed him in HANDCUFFS and threw him in the BACK of the squad car. Meanwhile, a woman was crying, "PLEASE don't TAKE my baby."

This time, it's evident the speaker didn't intend to step outside this day, and once he did, the police making the arrest was the last thing he expected to see. The story comes to life. As you develop as an artist, you will realize the value of cadence, the rise and fall of tone. It helps to drive a point home by stressing certain words. I want you to practice saying words at different volume levels for emphasis. Or, as the joke goes, put the right emPHASIS on the right sylLABle. Do this to change the context of different sentences. And when you rap, don't just rap monotone (the same pitch and volume level). Stretch words, distort them, even go so far as to cut them abruptly. Remember, as an emsee, you are also a musician, so think of what you do as an instrumentalist would think of their instrument. Your voice is the instrument, the words are the notes.

When I created the BARMONIC or TONEMIC system—a system for vocally representing different tones or pitches in order to make it easier to have multiple layers of vocal tracks or vocals in rap simultaneously—I based it on a system of *tones* or *pitch*. Though this system *is* based on some idea of music theory, its beginnings were more rooted in speech than in music. The topics covered thus far, especially those dealing with tone, pitch, and cadence, come directly from years of hard work that led to the creation of the barmonic/tonemic system.

The highness or lowness of the tone of your voice matters in rap. In the song "Stop being Greedy," DMX changes his tone (or pitch) every four bars, from a laid back or tamed tone to an aggressive tone, for the entirety of the song. When you think of tones or pitch in rap, there are some extremes examples we can use to show contrasting styles. Let's take Snoop, for example. Snoop raps with a very laid-back style. Snoop's vocal approach differs from Xzibit, whose voice and approach to rapping is very harsh and gritty, in terms of execution but also concerning the texture of Xzibit's voice. In music this is known as *timbre*.

Some emsees rap with more aggression and thus a harsher tone than others. Another example of contrasting style would be Bahamadia and Lady Luck. This is not to say these artists can't alternate; of course, they can. The point of these examples was to show the different uses of tone or pitch, a skill as important as verbal dexterity.

VERBAL DEXTERITY

VERBAL DEXTERITY IS about the art of syncopation, finding different rhythms inside of a rhythm and attacking a beat in order to make the music more interesting. Take, for example, Redman, who, on the 1998 track "Da Goodness," said,

> *The rhythm hit em without the venom in em*
> *Pen'll scare them with the sh*t I pull out the John Lennon*
> *Hah...*

If you try and say this to yourself very fast, you will be in the middle of a verbal dexterity storm. This takes practice and of course skill. If the rise and fall of your vocal pitch is tone or cadence, dexterity is the musicality of the rap, or the rhythmic pattern. So, if we return to the song "Genius Level Hip Hop" as an example, there's a phrase that goes:

> *Now I'm in the middle of a lot of mediocrity*
> *And everybody claiming that they gotta be*
> *A hot emcee to tell me*
> *And now they wanna tell me all you gotta do is ride the beat,*
> *It's all about the rhythm man I'm tellin' you it's gotta be....*

Phonetically, my flow is like a machine gun, or a snare playing 32nd notes, which gives the verse a lot of character and, above all, makes it more musical. Think of dexterity as the musicality of your rap and you want to try different approaches or different rhythmic patterns or syncopations. If you are going to demonstrate diversity as an artist, you don't want to use the same rhythmic pattern every time.

Some songs may require a completely different pattern, as in the Ntro to *A Lack of Convention*, where the lyrics go:

I remember working in the basement, while you were on a
slave ship
Couldn't take no more of the plantation.
I had to escape it, Django one chain with the language
and couldn't nobody tell me I ain't sick

Notice how the flow was not as aggressive and rapid-fire as "Genius Level Hip Hop," but what it did was create a vibe.

I remember working in the basement
while you were on a slave ship

In this example, the flow is constant, as with "Genius Level Hip Hop," but there are not as many syllables. There is a consistent rhythmic movement going on, but it's a different type of movement because there are fewer syllables. Again, think of dexterity as the musicality of your rap. To improve your dexterity, you will have to exercise patience. This is the part of rapping that may not be as glamorous, but it is what will separate you as an emsee from everyone else, who may be casual rappers. Practice being musical over a beat by using different flow patterns. You do this by letting the music play, and mumbling words over the music. Some of what you say may be nonsensical, some may make perfect sense. The goal is to find a rhythm, or several in the rhythm. You will listen to different raps from different regions to understand how these rhythms can vary. For example, Andre 3000 has a very complicated but choppy, almost robotic flow on the song "Chronomentrophia" from the *Idlewild* soundtrack, whereas Pharoahe Monch's flow (which is typically untypical) on "No Mercy," featuring M.O.P, changes throughout the verse. One approach is not better than the other. It really depends on the song and what you are trying to achieve. Andre 3000's song was more introspective and Pharoahe's was a show of his incredible technical skills as an emsee. In fact, both speak to the art of delivery or articulation.

ARTICULATION

SINCE I'VE DISCUSSED tones and dexterity, you are probably wondering what exactly is the difference between these and articulation? Well, ultimately, once you have all the poetic elements of rhyme structure and you can modulate your voice to the rhythm, then you must articulate or deliver all of this. This is the presentation or execution of your rap, i.e., how does the rap sound as a complete package when you rap to an audience or on a recording?

At this point, you want to listen to yourself. We all have a perceived voice in our heads. There's a voice of how we sound in our heads. When most people they hear themselves in a recording for the first time, they're always left with a puzzled look, asking, "Is that me?" Or, "Is that how I sound?"

I've been recording for years, and so I know how my outer voice sounds to others. I know how my voice sounds on recordings and what others will hear before a rap is even written. This is part of being an emsee, becoming one with your outer voice. I've mastered that outer voice and I understand all the nuances of this voice that most people will hear when they listen to me perform, or when they listen to one of my recordings. At this point, when I'm writing, I imagine that voice as opposed to the voice that I hear when I mouth or mumble phrases to the beat. People call this your head voice.

In order to become one with your outer voice, you must record yourself as often as possible. Get a device or get some recording software. Record yourself and listen to how you deliver your lyrics. Listen to the totality of your rap and master your outer voice by saying words slightly different and listening them. Try speaking and rapping at various volumes to see which tone of voice best fits you. Pay close attention to how you pronounce your words. Sometimes you may want to use the art of the slur, sometimes you want to be heavy when enunciating. You do this by paying attention to your tongue and teeth when you speak your words, even by changing the shape of your mouth. If you are trying to achieve precision and clarity with your words, saliva needs to be regulated.

I know we call rapping *spittin'* but it is important that saliva is regulated. You can't have too much saliva (or spit) in your mouth when you are going for precision and clarity. It must be the right amount. On the other hand, if your mouth is too dry, the dryness could cause your lips and tongue to stick to your gums, which will completely undermine your technique and ruin your performance. This drying up can happen from the adrenalin rush before a performance, so always be sure to drink plenty of water leading up to a performance. If you feel that you have too much saliva in your mouth, I have learned to balance this excess saliva with hot pepper. Obviously, you have to be careful using hot pepper, but when I was a teenager, I used a little hot pepper (jalapeño or any of the hot kind) to dry my tongue a little and even make it more lively, as pepper stimulates tongue movement.

Ultimately, it is important how you execute the elements you have learned. Note that some people sound better with an aggressive tone, such as DMX, Xzibit, or New Jersey emsee Rah Digga, while others sound better with the laid-back approach, such as Snoop, Bahamadia or Tierra Whack. How you articulate your rap is something for you to decide, but it is something you should take time to develop because it is the main thing that will distinguish you from others. The goal of any great artist is to find his or her own voice. You have something that is uniquely you, something that will give you your own place in history.

EMOTION

EQUALLY AS IMPORTANT as your technique on the mic will be your emotional approach. As an emsee, you have to be in tune with your emotions and the emotions of others, and learn to harness them. When you hear a beat, or a guitar lick, what emotion does either give you? Above all, what emotion are you trying to capture and convey? Tapping into your emotions as an emsee allows your art to make deeper connections with listeners. It is one thing to dazzle people with talent, but the rare emsees who make an emotional connection are the ones whose song will continue to play when the sound system is turned off.

Know that we are not solely our emotions. We are like a radio that picks up different frequencies, so whatever channel we are on will influence the style of music played or produced. Understanding this gives you more control of your emotions. And there is nothing wrong with emotions, or being emotional, despite the gangsta and tough guy image promoted in a lot of contemporary music. Emotions and feelings are what makes for great art.

Think of the full spectrum of human emotion and ask yourself where are you on that spectrum? Where do you want to be on this spectrum? You have to be very serious about the type of energy around you when you compose or record. If you are recording a sound about the loss of a loved one, you can't have people around you laughing and joking. Similarly, if you are trying to create from a place of joy, you have to dismiss someone presenting a contrary vibration. The emotional tone desired and achieved on a song matters as much as the song itself.

On "Been Around," YBN Cordae raps in a somber tone in order to communicate seriousness over some soulful guitar chord progressions. This tone of voice is typically used to draw focus to the lyrics of a verse. It makes sense musically because of the tempo and the very soulful chords. When you think of up-tempo or fast songs, think more energetic rap. When you think of mid-tempo or slower beats, think about calming your energy.

When you think of emotion in rap, it is important to think

of it the same way you would think of emotion in speech. When you are angry, what is your tone of voice? When you are sad, how does that sound? When the emsee is truly locked in with his or her emotions, they are paying attention to the mood of the track, and to the subject matter the song is trying to convey.

A person's delivery can set the tone of the song. The Fresh Prince rapped, "Parents just don't understand," as if he were reading a bedtime story to a child, or speaking to a group of children in a kindergarten class, whereas, on the song "U," Kendrick Lamar raps as if he's angry in the beginning, and then crying when the music changes.

If this sounds like the practice method for tones, it's because it is. Tones deal with pitch, or cadence, as does articulation. However, articulation deals with the overall execution of a rap, and how it comes across to the listener. There's a difference between what you hear in theory, and what will work in the performance of the rap.

6
FLOW

Rule: Learn to become one with the music

F LOW IS THE rhythmic sync of beat and lyrics. But crucial to this synchronization of beat and lyrics is the emsee becoming one with the rhythm. Don't just hear the hi-hat, *be* the hi-hat. Don't just hear the snare and rap to it, *be* so in sync with the snare that there is no separation between your timing and that of the drummer or drum machine. Each rhythm is a universe with counter rhythms and different pockets within the beat. Look for them.

When many first began rapping they assumed flow just comes through much trial and error. The truth is there's a teachable process. I learned this when I was fifteen. Another rapper I knew at the time wrote great lyrics, but when he delivered them, it was haphazard and unruly. He rambled, stopped, and started, and was not at all conscious of what was going on rhythmically. I had to slow the process down to explain to him what he was missing. So, let's again imagine the classic boom bap drum pattern. Focus. I'm going to give you a phrase we said when I was a kid:

My name is so and so. I'm here to say
I rap to the beat like every day.

To you, this may seem retro or dated, but it's the best starting point when learning how to rap on beat. If I were to take my name, O'hene Savánt, in the first iteration of this exercise, I would use one syllable. Let's say your name happens to be Kwame. Instead of saying "Kwame," I'd say "K" or "Kwam," to make it simpler. In my case, instead of saying "O'hene," I'd say, O, and so the phrase would go something like this:

My name is O. I'm here to say
I rap to the beat like every day.

Now, there's something happening here that I need you to focus on.

My^1 name^2 is^3 O^4, I'm^1 here^2 to^3 say^4
I^1 rap^2 to the^3 beat^4 like^1 ev^{2}ery^3 day^4

Now notice the last word (each "4") ends on the snare.

My^1 name^2 is^3 O^4, I'm^1 here^2 to^3 say^4
I^1 rap^2 to the^3 beat^4 like^1 ev^{2}ery^3 day^4

My^1 name^2 is^3 O^4, I'm^1 here^2 to^3 say^4
I^1 rap^2 to the^3 beat^4 like^1 ev^{2}ery^3 day^4

My^1 name^2 is^3 O^4, I'm^1 here^2 to^3 say^4
I^1 cringe^2 at^3 this^4 ex^1 am^{2}ple,^{3} but^4

...It works! The rhyme in that phrase all ended on the snare. I can't emphasize how important it is to remember this. You want any monosyllabic rhyme to end on the snare (the more advanced versions of that—a two-syllable or three-syllable rhyme—we'll get into later). Though said rhyme doesn't have to end on the snare, for there are no "rules" in art, I needed to provide you with the basics of rapping on beat in a recognized way. If you decide to break the rules, as I have done many times, then you'll be doing so with purpose, rather than stumbling upon a style that may sound dope but that you really can't control nor repeat. That is one of the keys to longevity and many emsees in the history of Hip Hop have demonstrated this.

ERAS OF FLOW

ON MY FIRST album, *The Rapademics*, I have a song where I go through the "eras of flow," from old school to new school, all the way to the tongue-twisting, or as some call it, the *choppa flow*, pioneered by the vocal acrobats Chip-Fu of the legendary group The Fu Schnickens and others like Twista. On my 2016 LP *First Millennial*, I also did part two of that song, where I broke the eras down in terms of flow types and organized them by decade.

I went from through the 1970s, 80s, 90s, 2000s, and 2010s. Perhaps you're familiar with the saying, "you can't know where you're going if you don't know where you've been." While overused, it really does ring true in this instance. It's important to study the history of your craft to not only keep up with the trends, but also to predict how things will evolve. Present forms of emseeing evolved from old school flow.

Old Skool Flow

Recall, I initially started with that very simple, foundational phrase:

> *My name is* O, *I'm here to* SAY
> *I rap to the beat like every* DAY.

This is modern rap in its infancy stages. This is how people rapped. In music theory, most of what you hear from rap predecessors like Pigmeat Markham are 8th notes and the space between words made this flow easier to grasp for casual rap listeners. Let's examine a section from Pigmeat Markham's "Here Comes the Judge":

> *Hear ye, hear ye, the court of* SWING
> *Is just about ready to do that* THING
> *I don't want no tears, I don't want no* LIES
> *Above all, I don't want no ali*BIS

The words that rhyme fall on the 2nd beat, which is where the snare typically lands in the funk tradition. This is important to know because Hip Hop is part of the Black music tradition, but specifically the funk music created by James Brown, Hip Hop's musical ancestor. Funk music is a soulful rhythmic style of music that places heavy emphasis on the first beat of 4 beats in a 4/4 time signature or, as it's known in the funk community, The ONE. Over the decades, rap and Hip-Hop production have never strayed from this emphasis of "The ONE."

Slowly, the old skool flow evolved by changing the cadence and adding more syllables or notes. For example, the above foundational phrase evolved into this old skool flow:

My name is O, *and well I'm here to* SAY
I be rappin' to the RHYTHM, *like ev-er-rey* DAY.

Try and say this to the same rhythm as before and be sure to have the rhymes land on the 2nd and 4th beat of the bar as before. As you write, find strategic parts in the song where you can replace shorter words with multisyllabic ones. In the simple, foundational phrase, instead of "my name is," try "ya'll know me as" and replace "I rap to" with "I be flowin' to," but notice how we consistently end with the words "say" and "day." It doesn't matter what you do in between; as long as you end on the same note with the same syllable, you won't break the rhythm or the rhyme scheme.

New Skool Flow

The new skool flow introduced more syllables but added those syllables over the 2nd and 4th beat in a 4/4 time signature song. For example, on Spoonie Gee and Kool Moe Dee's "New Rap Language," Spoonie Gee raps:

> *Well I'm Spoonie Gee, as you could see*
> *I rock the whole society*
> *I always rock, as you can tell*
> *I rock with all the clientele*
> *Finesse is do you know I will*
> *I keep the people staring still*
> *Eyes swollen, rhymes tolling*
> *Coming out this microphone*

Then Kool Moe Dee comes in:

> *Remember me, MC Moe Dee*
> *The man that's at the T-O-P*
> *A ladies dream the way it seem*
> *When they see me, their eyes are gleaming*
> *I'm so shocking when I'm rocking*
> *Bound to get your fingers popping*
> *Have no doubt, I turn it out*
> *'Cause that's a party's all about*

These new skool verses differ from the old skool approach because the flow is structured for the rhythm of the words to be continuous by using a "1-2-3" rhythmic pattern that plays out as 16th notes instead of 8th notes, which is a notch faster. Compare lines, side-by-side, from "Here Comes the Judge" [1] and the "New Rap Language" [2]:

[1] *Hear ye, hear ye, the court of* SWING
[2] *Spoonie Gee, as you could see*
I rock the whole society

The new skool flow as embodied by the "New Rap Language" uses multi-syllable rhyming so the rhyme takes up more time on the 2nd beat.

Let's examine this flow further and identify the beats on which the words land, in order to better understand how this flow was structured. Remember, after the 4th beat ends, we return to 1st, or as Godfather of Soul James Brown taught us, "The ONE."

Well I'm
(1) Spoonie Gee, as
(2) you could see, I
(3) rock the whole so
(4) ciety, I
(1) always rock, as
(2) you can tell, I
(3) rock with all the
(4) clientele

Notice that this flow is more rhythmic, more musical. Also note a critical difference between old and new skool flows: new skool rappers added syllables where the snare landed on the 2nd and the

4th beat, and so Pigmeat used 8 syllables per bar, whereas Spoonie Gee used 15 syllables per bar or measure.

Emsees began blending more with the music. There was a plan. In an earlier time, an emsee would simply show up to a performance with little previous thought and crafted a few basic lines onto whichever breakbeat the DJ selected. By this era, I imagine the emsee and DJ collaborated ahead of time. They probably went over some breakbeats together, which allowed the emsee to plan out his or her rhymes. As a result, the art form took one step closer to the written and recorded rap song.

During this evolution, rap bars went from 16th note to the 32nd syncopation, adding syllables and adding musicality. The innovator and genius Kool Mo Dee helped rap evolve rhythmically with the song "New Rap Language." This song was released by his group, The Treacherous 3, who inspired the rapper Treach from Naughty by Nature. Treach and groups like Leaders of the New School modernized the rhythmic technique of rapping for their time period by changing the cadence and some of the rhyme schemes.

This is what I hope you take from this lesson: There have been emsees before you and there will be some after you. If you truly love rap, you will love the work of those who loved it before you and you will study them. This is important. Treach is not Treach without the Treacherous 3. 2Pac is not 2Pac without Chuck D and Ice Cube. We all have predecessors. We are also part of a continuum, whether it be Sarkodie and M.anifest growing up listening to Reggie Rockstone, or the Notorious B.I.G being influenced by Heavy D. Artists like Pigmeat Markham and Grand Master

Melle Mel have impacted all my influences as well as yours, no matter when you picked up this book or decided to rap. Through the craft of rap, we are all part of one big family as emsees.

Tongue Twist or Chopper Flow

After the "New Rap Language," the pioneers of Hip Hop continued to test the limits and musicality of rap by adding syllables, proceeding from a 16th note approach to an even faster 32nd note execution, thus speeding up the verse's delivery known as twisting, choppin' or double timing. This approach stretched the limits of what could be accomplished in a bar. There are several who pioneered the era of tongue twisting. In the late 1980s, Heavy D used the triplet scat "diddley diddley D," originally heard on Masters of Ceremony's 1986 song "Sexy," while Hip-Hop legend Jaz O became a tongue twist pioneer, highlighted by the 1990 song "The Originators. In 1991-92, Das Efx used intricate rhymes with an"iggidy" flow that built upon the triplet effect. Other innovative rappers of the era include Tung Twista (later known as Twista) and Chip Fu of the Fu Schnickens. On the 1991 Fu Shnickens song, "True Fu Shnick," Chip Fu raps:

I'm a rowdidy rowdy piper I flash my dread Sherlock Holmes
The thicker the richer the bigger the dread
So I don't need no honeycomb
So eeney, meeney, miney, mo good goobelly goo I bumped my
toe
Oh-oh, "oh-oh better get Maoco" chocolate Chip's about to
flow

The super the cola the fraja the listic expialadope Chip
When the mic is gripped in ridobidobip bip da be bong de
dang, Bo!
'No worries and boderations when I raps it up again and
again and again
But not with the same FU style I'm wicked and wild and
versatile

If we were to slow Chip Fu's flow down, it exhibits triplets or the use of 3 notes or words stacked together. But let's look closer at the 8th line in Chip Fu's verse, where he decides to double the time of his flow:

No worries and boderations when I raps it up again and
again and again (21)

At 102 beats per minute, Chip Fu rapped 21 syllables in 1 bar or measure. Do you notice a pattern here, in the evolution of flow? Perhaps a comparison will make this pattern clearer: Pigmeat Markham used 8 syllables, Spoonie Gee used 15 syllables, and Chip Fu used 21 syllables per bar.

Using the basics outlined thus far, you will grasp how to execute flows from each era but you will also need to listen to them. This exercise is as much an audible experience as it is a visceral experience, so take the time to engage the flows of different eras and do it objectively. If you approach listening to these eras with humility, you will rid yourself of generational biases and will also evolve as an emsee in ways you never imagined.

Triplet or Stutter Flow

Throughout the decades, Hip Hop production continued to evolve, and the southern region of the United States contributed a sub-genre called Trap. This era created an emphasis on the "triplet flow." Although the triplet flow is a readily used one in the 2010 era, the Dismasters's 1987 song "Small time Hustler" and Public Enemy's "Bring the Noise" from Hip-Hop legend Chuck D released that year both used the triplet approach. There have been many who have used the triplet flow, ranging from Three 6 Mafia, Bone Thugs N Harmony and Tommy Wright III in the 1990s. Indeed, this triplet flow that has become a staple in rap and has created its own line of innovators, such as the Migos.

Although used by an entire generation of rappers and emsees, it is important to indicate where or how this style differs from traditional forms. The triplet flow uses 3 words or notes closely paired together in succession but this flow also makes use of spacing and multi-syllable rhyming in a unique way. For example, on Eric B. and Rakim's "Paid in Full," Rakim's verse begins with the line, "Thinking of a master plan," which starts on the first beat. The first syllable literally drops on the first beat, on "The ONE." For Migos, in the song "Movin' too Fast," you will notice that the first syllable is said on the 2nd beat:

(*1*) _____ (*2*) *I put the streets on beat*

The first beat (or "The ONE") is left empty. This is quite normal, though it doesn't always happen, but it is very much a staple for many triplet style rappers. Rhymes using this approach tend to be multi-syllabic and extend beyond the first beat of the snare. You will also notice that the triplet flow incorporates extra syllables at the end of the triplet. Let's highlight this feature in the example below, by capitalizing the extra syllables used. In "The Search," NF says:

BEEN MAKIN A WHOLE LOT OF CHANGES
WROTE A SONG ABOUT THAT YOU SHOULD PLAY IT
I GET SCARED WHEN I WALK ON THESE STAGES
I look at the crowd and see so many FACES
Yeah
That's when I start to get ANXIOUS
That's when my thoughts can be DANGEROUS
That's when I put on my makeup
And drown in self-hatred forget what I'm SAYIN AN

You'll notice that the triplet is used in conjunction with carefully placed syllables in such a way that, at times, help to start the triplet flow and yet, at other times, are there to help finish it.

Offbeat Flow

These lessons on the eras of flow are based on what has been standard flows throughout for years. However, there have been those who have, for decades, created around these standards. If you've ever listened to Rza or Suga Free and at times E 40, you will have heard their "offbeat" style and understood a creative art form in what—from a distance—may sound like rambling. Anyone who studies rhythm will notice that there is a method to the apparent madness. I've studied all flows and approaches, and have, at times, also incorporated offbeat flow into my catalog.

Bop Rap or Free Flow

Rap flows have gone through many transitions and one of my childhood dreams was to add to the flow repertoire of rap. Bop Rap or Free Flow is that contribution. Since the beginning of Hip Hop, rap has been confined to loops, typically in 4/4 time signature. This pop music approach to time signatures is something I have challenged since the start of my career with the 2003 "Waltz in O minor" (in 3/4 time) from my boom bap album, *The Rapademics*. Anyone who knows my story or who has listened to my interviews understand that my father Stevenson A. Williams is a classical pianist virtuoso, and so Western classical music was a big part of my childhood. Shortly after my first album, I began to experiment with this classical music more and eventually Bebop. It was my moments with said classical music and Bebop that challenged my thinking about rap and how I wanted to approach it.

I'm part of a tradition that traces its evolution from radio DJ and Hip-Hop pioneer Douglass "Jocko" Henderson and renaissance man Sammy Davis Jr., who rapped triplets over jazz music in the 1950 song "Sam's Song." In this tradition of jazz and rap, we find an evolving rap-jazz fusion from groups like A Tribe Called Quest, De La Soul, Gangstar and Guru's multi-volume Jazzamataz to the Freestyle Fellowship, who stretched the boundaries of Hip-Hop jazz fusion. Growing up in Hip Hop, I've been directly or indirectly influenced by many of the artists and groups in this book. Since the beginning of my career, however, I found myself frustrated with the conventions of popular music, these being the standard 4/4 time and "the loop" (music that repeats the same phrase consistently throughout a song). Out of this frustration I created the Bop Rap or Free Flow Rap. Bop Rap is unmetered or free rhythm, but it also uses what I have called, and referred to earlier as, the "Barmonic system" or "Barmony." This is not rap-jazz fusion; all these elements constitute rhythmic symphony.

My father is one of the most disciplined men I know and I strongly believe his high standards shaped me, and for which I am grateful. In 2005 I created a song, "Cat Daddy," that was the first iteration of Free Flow. I would later learn more about the culture of Bebop under the mentorship of the legendary James Mtume, son of Jimmy Heath of the legendary Bebop group, The Heath Brothers. But my childhood and artistic vision all came together on the song "Rap Opera" (the first 30-minute rap song) in 2012 and on "Not so Brilliant Corners," recorded in 2009 and released in 2013. On these songs I freed rap from the loop. This is why the scene 7 in Rap Opera says:

> *I...I am free from the loop,*
> *I am out of the loop,*
> *oops, now I am Bruce,*
> *who's Bruce?*
> *Bruce Lee...*

When you listen to this portion of the song, you will notice that it has no time signature and no tempo. This is completely meterless rap, thus the name Free Flow. I reference Bruce Lee in this segment of the song because it was a goal of Bruce Lee to synchronize all of the complexities of the different martial arts forms into one, simplified martial art form, *Jeet Kune Do* ("The way of the intercepting fist"). Free flow is rhythmically fluid and doesn't adhere to the traditions of staccato or 8th, 16th and 32nd note that has been the approach to rap for over three decades. There are times where free flow goes so far as to sustain a note (or word) for half a bar (in music theory, a half note) and even the whole bar (or whole note). In order for rap to have evolved past its dance oriented or pop formula, it needed to go outside the conventions of popular music. In doing so, an entirely new universe becomes available and its own community and industry will develop, once it is understood the way Western classical and Bebop music is now understood. As an emsee, this is my vision.

SPACE AND PAUSES FOR EFFECT

THERE IS SOMETHING significant about silence, pausing for it or creating a space for it. In music, silence can be as important as the music itself. Hip Hop comes out of an urban environment where there is always something going on. This doesn't necessarily mean that all rap is the product of a noisy environment. Rap should reflect the subways but also the mountains, the hood as well as the meadows, making it a truly universal form of expression. For the emsee, we must listen to the spaces and gaps in the music and learn the power of absence to make presence more potent. Listen to the silence and use it.

The significance of this spacing and pausing for effect is well illustrated by Scarface, who, some time ago, said:

Day by day it's more impossible to cope,
I feel like I'm the one that's doing dope

Instead of filling up the full four beats, he leaves one beat open. He deliberately stops rapping at the third beat to leave room for reflection. This is a classic example of emotional spacing for effect. Scarface was not insincere in his rap; the pause was perfectly timed and caused the listener to reflect.

There are other examples, such as A Tribe called Quest's "Bonita Applebum." Qtip leaves the first beat open and comes in with only two beats worth of lyrics. At the time, this was groundbreaking because rap had traditionally filled such spaces with lyrics. It took innovative thinkers like Tribe to understand that there should be no outright barriers when it comes to song structure. In the first verse of "I Wonder," Kanye West only uses between eight and nine syllables per measure or bar:

I've been waiting on this my whole life (9)
These dreams be waking me up at night (9)
You say I think I'm never wrong (8)
You know what, maybe you're right, aight (8)

To help you understand how radical this verse is, Ludacris' "Do your Time" has 57 syllables, Logic's "Pardon my Ego" has 45, and Joey Bada$$'s "Piece of Mind" has 50 syllables in the first bar. Understanding rap composition, we can then turn to getting these verses out of our heads and into the hands of Hip-Hop fans.

PERFORMANCE

Recording

I have called my music the "museum of my soul," because recording is not just about laying vocals. Let's think about the word "record-ing" and ask what are you recording? What is it you bring to the table that is worth being recorded? Historically, recording has been used to document important information for future generations. In today's world and in my case, I am documenting the totality of my being, the very things that animates me. My personality, my energy, my laugh, my anger, even my bitterness. Whenever I step to a microphone, I am seeking to archive a part of myself that will not be available forever. Think carefully about how you want to record yourself, how you want to be documented. These considerations will make the technical process of recording more meaningful.

Every rapper should aspire to have their own home studio. Most readers are familiar with the studio basics: a microphone, a desktop computer, recording hardware and software, and some sort of soundproofing. Let's begin with a couple seemingly small details you may have overlooked the last time you were in a commercial studio. The circular thin layered foam inches from the mic is called a pop filter. A pop filter stops a lot of the hard-consonant sounds like "B," "K," and "P" from creating a popping noise when pronounced a bit too hard. Those strong consonant sounds cause distortion in mixes and end up messing up a mix during post-production. Simply put, get one. If you can't afford it, you can make one from a coat hanger and some stockings or some speaker mesh. Just bend the top of the coat hanger into a loop, bottom part straight (this should look like a balloon with a string tied to it) and cover the loop with the stockings or speaker mesh. The loop should not be large (just big enough to cover the microphone). The microphone should fit in the middle of the loop with enough space around the mic for you to draw an invisible circle.

I would have an area of focus right behind your mic stand. Some artists like to use a mirror. Others have a poster of their musical heroes or certain goals written out in some form. While this is not needed, it can add extra inspiration, as a reminder why you emsee/rap when get tired, during those late-night sessions into sunrise sessions.

There are so many other pieces of equipment you can add to your home studio, but it all depends on your needs. Look up "MIDI," "compressor" and "pre-amp," for starters. Watch a few tutorials online and discuss it with other artists in your inner circle before rushing into a purchase. Recording software will come with dozens of features and add-ons. Make sure you play with all these features to make sure you're getting the most out of your recordings but be sure to run these experiments past trusted ears before releasing the music. It may sound great to you, but keep in mind, part of your appreciation may be teaching yourself how to use a specific effect, not because that effect made the song better.

When you're recording vocals, one of the things to remember is the distance or proximity between you and the microphone. I've taught you the distance between the microphone and your mouth. If you need a refresher, check out some videos of me in the studio. You will notice my pop filter is just about where the thumb would.

Proximity

Proximity is about where you are positioned in relation to the microphone. This is a lesson that most have not understood. As someone who has mastered the art of recording, I have learned how to translate my ideas in ways that are often new to rap. The concept of proximity is not something you will hear in Hip Hop circles, but the craft of emseeing requires that we discuss it. Rapping is not only about what you say, but how you say it. It is also about where you say it and where you are when you say it. Think about it: if I wanted to tell you a secret, I would typically lean in and whisper in your ear. Well, how would this idea work in a recording? We get closer to the microphone. The closer you are to the microphone, the more intimate you will appear. The further away, the more distant you'll appear. If you listen to my recordings, you will notice I use this proximity technique regularly. For the more aggressive songs, I am not as close to the microphone, but for the more intimate ones, I am. I came up with a simple formula to remember: LFSC, which stands for LOUD FAR, SOFT

CLOSE. Remember this formula and don't record vocals without understanding the value of proximity.

When capturing your lyrics, don't be afraid to take multiple takes. Some rappers love to brag about one take and getting it right the first time. Don't feel pressed by this. First, this is Hip Hop, the world of hype, so many of them are stretching the truth. Some clever editing could make it seem they walked right into the studio from the streets, spit a rhyme, then walked right out. Watching at home, you have no way of knowing how many takes it took to make that "one take" video. Second, it's not as if fans will find out or even care. I have also never heard someone say they liked a song any less because they found out the rapper rerecord his vocals twenty times to get that perfect take. But, if getting things done in one take is your way, that's okay as well. I've worked with the genius Chubb Rock, who records all his music in one take and has for his entire career. He likens himself to a jazz musician; he has set that standard for himself. He does this exceptionally well and to the point you would never know otherwise. And yet, that's not everyone. If your work requires some serious scrutiny, it's okay. Do what works to bring out the best emsee in you. Once the verses are recorded, you will need to lay the *overdubbing*.

Overdubbing

Overdubbing is a concept that came out years ago in Hip Hop, where you highlight certain portions of an already recorded verse by recording those parts again and playing both simultaneously. I, for example, had a song on my first album where I said:

I'm a lyrical scientist in a musical lab
Trying to etch out hieroglyphs in unusual math

An effective way to overdub is to record that rap, then come back on another "track" and highlight the "-tist" in scientist, "lab," the "-glyphs" in hieroglyphs and "math" by saying each these words again, and even in a different tone. By the way, recording "tracks" are lines of recording that run simultaneously; imagine an actual track with four Olympic sprinters side by side all running at the same time. In our case, the runners are your vocals, your overdubs, the beat, and the effects; instead of competing, their goal to all cross the finish line at the same time, but in a way that is aesthetically pleasing to the audience.

Overdubbing is a very important and yet overlooked element by most rappers. Part of rap's evolution is directly linked to overdubbing. For example, I coined the concept of the BAR-MONIC STRUCTURE or BAR-MONY, where raps are charted out and delivered in thirds. As in the note or pitch or tones, the third is four steps above a root note, in that it goes up four semitones from the root note. Some of my innovations flow directly from the bar-monic structure or bar-mony concept. The bar-monic structure or bar-mony uses overdubs that are spread out over a landscape of varying tones (which helps to create the separation of the voices) to produce a bed of background vocals that act independently of the lead vocals. This is a new concept to rap. But to help us out, listen to the following songs from my catalog: "Cesare Borgia," "Rap Opera" (a 30-minute song) or "B/" and "Not so Brilliant Corners."

Overdubbing should not be confused with *ad-libbing*, which is similar but slightly different in approach. When you are overdubbing, you are typically adding a layer of the same thing over the lead vocal (called *stacking*); however, when you are ad-libbing, you could make the stacked vocal say something different than the lead vocal and you are normally looking for spaces between the rhyme to jump in. Think of ad-libbing as you would in a live performance setting. When you watch the performance of a rap, you will typically see the rapper and another person on the stage backing them. That other person doesn't do most of the rap; the person backing just highlights certain parts of the rap, and waits for empty space in the rhyme where he or she can chime in. A lot of 1990s-era rap used overdubbing and you hear ad-libbing more so in 2010 era rap. Overdubbing and ad-libbing are not a necessity, but when used properly, they can be secret weapons in your arsenal!

Punch-ins

A *punch-in* is something we need to discuss, although it is not needed for a song. It is an enhancement, and if used properly, could serve as an aid and give a lot more character to your verse. There will be times where it makes sense to use the multitrack option to lay different parts of your verse on a song. For example, you may be telling a story, and want to use an additional track to do a back and forth type of verse, almost as if you were talking to someone in a conversation, or they were chiming in and asking questions about what you are rapping about. Earlier in his career, Eminem did this quite a bit. For example, in the song "The Real Slim Shady," he raps,

> *You think I give a damn about a* GRAMMY?
> *Half of you critics can't even stomach me, let alone* STAND
> ME
>
> **"But Slim, what if you win,**
> **wouldn't** ***it be weird*****?"**
>
> *Why? So you guys could just lie to* GET ME HERE?
> *So you can,* SIT ME HERE *next to* BRITNEY SPEARS?

The punch-in is the part in BOLD.

A punch-in is normally done in a different pitch to add to the effect. This is not something that you have to do, and some emsees prefer not to do anything in the studio he or she can't perform live. It is therefore entirely up to you, as to how you approach punch-ins. Some use punch-ins to make their flow better in recordings by completing phrases they were unable (for whatever reason) to complete. I use punch-ins to give variety mainly to my vocal performances. It creates a break in tone and vocal styling.

7
LIVE PERFORMANCE

Rule: Learn the art of dramatization. Learn to master presentation on stage and on the mic

T HE LIVE PERFORMANCE leaves the artist metaphorically naked and his or her mind flooded with a range of thoughts and emotions. Before I go onto any stage, there is always a lot going on in my head. I think of my inner and outer voices to help quiet the many other voices I hear. The family member who told you that you weren't good enough, or the troll online who told you to quit because you didn't have "the look" to "make it." There are also voices of genuine concern, coming from a pure place, advising you to do something you had no intention of doing for your performance. I recall the mantra I created, and quiet the storm before I hit the stage. Without the aid of the various shortcuts and the ability to do retakes, as in the studio, putting energy into live performance early make for a stronger artist later. All live performances start with body control and bodily expressions.

BODY LANGUAGE

THE AUDIENCE IS watching your facial expressions; they are checking out your clothes and hair. If these things aren't pleasing to the eye, then you could lose their attention. In the moment, this can even be more important than the words you speak. Even though talent is the most important part of your presentation, imagine a rapper at a concert whispering about his lady in a monotone voice, compared to someone rapping with charisma about their queen! Who do you think will get a greater response from the audience?

Always remember, you must sell the presentation and selling is about body language. Watch your shoulders. They need to be open and broad, not slouched, so you project confidence. Crossing your arms communicates impatience. Constantly touching your face could tell everyone that you're self-conscious about how you look. Always rap with your head up, your chin up, and speak with confidence. Use your head—I mean this literally. Learn how to *lean in* when you want to project authority, and when to lean back or look to the side while rapping. All of this adds to the overall performance.

In addition, you should always make sure your clothes are as dope as possible, and your style makes sense according to your brand (the image you are trying to project). It's important to stress what you wear does not make or break you as an artist. And yet, be conscious of your look and take it seriously. Although Hip Hop is the place to be yourself, know that almost everything is and can be recorded. I've seen some artists purposefully wear their unclean work uniform on stage. They do this to appear more relatable, under the impression fans want their favorite artist to seem just like them. I disagree. From what I've seen, fans look up to their favorite artist, and some aspire to be like them. And it is my position that artists should represent excellence (as much as possible) and give the people something positive to pursue. Fulfill that fantasy for your fans. Show them that you have taken time in all aspects of your presentation. Not taking time to think about your wardrobe doesn't make you more authentic. I'm not suggesting you must wear expensive jewelry and very expensive gear (especially if you speak out against that in your music), but that there is a world of fashion between designer and cheaper apparel.

THE EYES

THERE IS A saying that "the eyes are the mirrors of the soul," or "windows to the soul." Your eyes communicate a lot. Be mindful of the message your eyes send. If as the saying goes, "A person's thoughts can be ascertained by looking in his or her eyes," we say a lot with our eyes, whether we know it or not. People are looking at your body language as much as they are listening to your words, and as an emsee you are also a public speaker. Be sure to project the appropriate message with your eyes. Think about it: if you are trying to project anger, would it make sense to squint your eyes? No. That may make sense for a suspicious look, not anger. I want you to pay attention to facial expressions in general and the eyes specifically. Learn the art of the glance and sometimes make your eyes move to the rhythm. Learn when to squint and when to widen your eyes based on the mood of the song or the moment you have in mind.

GESTURING

As an emsee, *gesturing* is thing you should take the time to practice. These are the hand movements you make while rapping. Think of gesturing as the art of hand and non-verbal dramatization.

When you look at most emsees or rappers in general, you will notice they typically do something with their hands. A friend and fellow emcee E Snipe made this dope observation about rappers gesturing while rapping in order to keep the beat or timing. That was a great observation. Although I've never approached gesturing for timing purposes, I could see that being the case. For me, gesturing is a part of the performance aesthetic; in other words, I use it for effect. When I am using very elaborate phrases or doing a twist or chopper flow, I will normally gesture along with the vocal performance. I also dramatize lyrics with my hands during my performance. Use hand gestures to drive home your points, just as any other public speaker would. When you want to speak with authority, you may point. When you want to convey sadness, you may grab your head. This is a very important part of emceeing, so practice this in the mirror. Also, practice gesturing to the rhythm of your rhyme. Lift your hand, and move it to every syllable you say, and stop on every pause. This will make for a more theatrical performance.

HOW TO HOLD THE MIC

A DEAD GIVEAWAY to a rapper's professionalism (or lack there-of) is how he or she holds the microphone. The average concert goer probably thinks, "Oh, it's just the microphone. You can grab it anywhere." Rappers have a bad reputation for either holding the mic too close to their mouths or cupping the mic (covering the part of the microphone into which you speak). It's possible these bad habits come from an attempt to overcompensate for poor-quality sound equipment. When I first returned to Philadelphia from Ghana, I performed in some places with some subpar mics and speakers. Most of you will do the same; this is part of paying your dues. Imagine playing soccer with a partially deflated soccer ball on an uneven grassy field. You would have to kick the ball much harder than usual to make it go as far as you need. Now, imagine having grown up with these restrictions as part of your normal reality. Even a protege with World Cup-level ability would have a difficult time dealing with these habits developed over the years.

To practice proper spacing the mic from your lips, grab the closest mic-shaped object you can find. If you've yet to begin work on your home studio, and you don't have an actual mic, grab a hairbrush, a TV remote, or even a candlestick. Open the hand in which you'll hold the mic (typically, the hand with which you write), as if you are about to shake someone's hand. With your other hand, put the mic or object next to your palm, with your fingers still straight and your thumb still in the handshake position. Begin to wrap your index, middle, ring, and pinky around the mic leaving your thumb still pointed up. Make sure the windscreen (top of the mic or object) is slightly protruding at the top of your palm where your thumb is. (An ineffective way to handle the mic would be to cover the windscreen, known as cupping.) Now, tilting the mic back towards your lips, with your thumb still pointed up, the space between your mouth and the mic is the correct distance. This measurement is a good way to gauge appropriate distance, giving you enough proximity for clarity on the mic. At this proximity, we will be able to hear all the words you speak or rap.

If you practice how much space you'll need between your mouth and the mic, this spacing will begin to feel natural, and you'll no longer need your empty hand to find the placement. If you lose this spacing mid-performance, stick out the thumb of the hand holding the mic. The thumb distance between your mouth and the actual microphone is a rough equivalence. Without proper distance, your words enter the mic too quickly and thus sounds distorted through the speakers. Alas, if your lyrics are terrible and you don't want the audience to hear them, I suggest you continue holding the mic close. However, if you got this far in the book, I'm certain you've mastered or you are working on mastering lyricism. Knowing how to hold the mic and how to gesture leads us naturally to a discussion of the venue.

THE VENUE

WHEN YOU THINK of a performance, there are many things that come to mind. Sometimes you think of arenas, sometimes you may imagine a stadium. It all depends how big the event. I have performed in events as big as 50,000 and as small as 5 or 6 people. All of these are valuable and there are lessons to be learned in each. In a performance with just a few people, it is important to think more intimately. I never use a microphone in that instance because it takes away from the intimacy of such a performance. In other words, it creates a distance between you the performer and the audience. In the more glamorous setting (the arena or stadium), I have learned that it's better to focus on the performance from a stage perspective. The audience is so large that making an intimate connection is nearly impossible. Typically, barriers will block the audience from the stage. The larger the audience, the louder you will need your microphone to be. I have lost my voice trying to compete with the intensity of tens of thousands of people screaming at the same time. Different performance venues have different challenges. One such challenge is the acoustics of the building if you are indoors. I have performed inside of churches and even gyms and it is very difficult to hear lyrics when your voice is drowning in the echoes of the room. Sound travels and, depending on how the venue was built, the sounds could bounce back and forth between the walls of the venue in a way that obstructs your lyrics.

Sometimes this kind of obstruction is just too difficult to address, unless the room is treated with sound absorbers and that is something the venue owner would have to address. You can, however, move around in the room and have a friend listen from different parts of the room to see from which part your rap sound better. Just know that the environment where the performance will take place is important. When you are coming up, the venues will be less appealing but that is part of your development, so don't look down on the process. The grind will teach you valuable lessons about ingenuity and you will develop the skill of working through difficult times. Outside performances are sometimes challenging because there are normally environmental factors you will have to deal with. There could be vehicles passing, people talking as they walk by or it could even begin raining. For every street performance I've done, I always made it a point to bring the audience in closer, which touches on a major point of live performances.

MOVE THE CROWD

ALWAYS CONTROL THE crowd. When you hear this, it sounds like the Hip Hop cliché, "Move the crowd." To move the crowd emotionally is always important, but sometimes you may have to literally move the crowd. I do this all the time. If I am looking for a more intimate experience, I will tell the audience to come closer or I will go to them. Listening to the acoustics of the venue or noticing there are many distractions during an outside performance, you may need to literally move the crowd.

THE STAGE

AS THE EMSEE, it may or may not be your responsibility to ensure the rest of the stage is set up correctly. However, if you think about it, as a performing artist, your songs *are* the product. If an improperly placed speaker, microphone feedback, or poor stage light prevents the audience from enjoying your concert, they are going to blame *you*! So please, make sure you have everything that you need. Make sure the DJ or sound engineer has your instrumentals. These days, that can be done via email, but you may wish to bring a flash drive as backup for corrupted files, bad Wi-Fi connection, or even the sound man forgetting his password (try to cover all possibilities, because the audience will hold you responsible). Do a walk-through of the venue as early as possible (a day or two) before the concert. Make sure all the cables are properly connected.

Introduce yourself to the sound and lighting crew. Talk to them about your priorities. If it's a college campus, the students will probably be excited to work with you and be willing to experiment with different setups. Whatever props you're going to use, make sure everything is cataloged. The best way to do that is to make a list. Keep this list available for everyone to see during rehearsal, so that everyone knows their role and their responsibilities. There's nothing more upsetting than planning an entire performance around certain props brought on stage in a certain order, and then have them not appear on cue. My song "Bastard Child" fades to a clip of Dr. Cornel West discussing what he appreciates about my music. If I were to perform this live, I might have an actor dressed as Dr. West appear from off stage, lip-syncing his words. Now, imagine if I forgot to bring the wig for the actor to depict Dr. West's distinctive afro. The reference would probably be lost. At minimum, the audience would be robbed of that half a minute of wondering, "Wait a minute, is that *actually* Dr. West?"

Prepare days or even weeks in advance, depending on the length of your set. If only a one-song talent show, always rehearse as much as possible in advance, while an hour-long concert will probably require a lot of nightly rehearsals. Don't forget to record your rehearsal so you can watch it from the audience's perspective. You might also catch a clip worthy of a viral moment, if something spontaneous, hilarious, or exciting happens.

Of course, you don't want to micromanage or come off as disregarding. Always respect the sound engineer, DJ, light technician, bartender, and venue security as the professionals they are. The more you know about each aspect of concert promotion, the more you can add each of these aspects into your show, and in ways that enhance or make it more enjoyable, which is ultimately what you are there to do. On the surface, it may seem the only purpose a security guard serves is to bar entry to anyone carrying a weapon, underaged (in the case of venues that cater to adults) or did not purchase a ticket.

And yet, a good relationship with security can uncover some creative approaches that will strengthen the show. For example, security can help make sure your most supportive fans will be front and center when you perform, by letting them know the exact moment, according to the show schedule, you will hit the stage. Said fans can therefore time their bathroom and snack break accordingly. These fans should be easily identifiable by their t-shirts or hats with your logo; by the way, you should *have* t-shirts and hats. In addition, perhaps while checking IDs, security notices someone's birthday. If the relationship is there, they can text you this information, and you can give one lucky fan a most unexpected birthday shout-out, guaranteeing this person is now a fan for life.

Live performances require multitasking. While most of your energy will be devoted to delivery of your lyrics, you also want to pay attention to what's happening while on stage. How is the audience receiving you? Are people smiling and singing along, live blogging via social media, or grimacing in a way that indicates they are having trouble hearing you? Each of these requires a different response. Despite countless hours of rehearsal, you must also remain flexible. In a live show, anything can happen. Someone might start heckling you in the middle of your set. The point here is that there is no one appropriate response to any of these scenarios. You must take advantage of opportunities as they arise. Once, I was accompanying gospel harpist Jeff Majors at a concert in a North Carolina arena, as we had recently collaborated on his single "Trying Times." The lineup also including Mary J. Blige and gospel singers Mary Mary. The place was packed. When we hit the stage, the voice mics worked, but there were some glitches with the computer and so the programmed music didn't play. The crowd started to get restless, so I took advantage of this opportunity to spit an *off the top*. The crowd was so into it, they didn't notice the sound engineer giving the "all ready" signal for the scheduled events to continue.

Regardless of the unexpected events you will run into, begin and end your set punctually. Don't delay the first song with a long introduction. Your core fans already know who you are. Concert goers who aren't fans yet will be won over with the music. So, make sure that first song hits hard! Likewise, end on a strong note. This will be the audience's last impression, and if you are opening for a more popular act, this will be their first impression. If you go over your scheduled time, surely the main act will be left with a negative impression because you kept them and their fans waiting.

Don't be afraid to break what they call in stage plays, "the fourth wall." Sometimes in smaller venues I like to walk out into the audience. The intimacy this creates help them focus on me and absolutely shuts up any haters and hecklers. Depending on my mood, I might get right in their face, sending the message, "you over here pretending you could get at me in a battle rap, but you don't really want it!" At other times, I might stand next to them, then turn my back on them, à la Miles Davis. This sends the equally powerful message that I care more about those who appreciate my music, and I won't waste any time with a hater. But that's just for hecklers, which, thankfully, I tend not to have.

Most of your focus should be on delivery, but also be conscious of more than just your mouth. Keep in mind, the audience craves a visual experience. Therefore, they're watching your overall presentation.

Part of my hope in sharing these seven principles of rap with you is that you will study, and in due course share the techniques you've discovered with future generations, so the artform of emseeing will continue to grow. These methods have worked for me, my entire career, so if you study and use them, I'm sure they'll do the same for you. Rap is a medium. It is as much of a musical expression as playing a violin or piano. It requires time and discipline, as does any craft, so study it and take it seriously. And above all, know that this is a powerful artform, so use it wisely and give back with your content.

Over the years, I have taught many, and the one thing I wish I had taught, more than how to rap, was rapping with purpose and the power of this art. Or, how to use rap to make a positive difference in the lives of others. I thank you for joining me and all emsees on this journey, and congrats on becoming an EMSEE! Now, let's transform the world for the better!

Much love and B/

SHOUT OUTS

BEFORE I BEGIN with these shout outs, let me emphasize that I cannot even begin to thank everyone who has been a part of my journey. I'm certain I will unintentionally leave someone out and beat myself up for it, so, in advance, I apologize to anyone omitted. I am an individual who comes from the village that it takes to raise a child and raising me was no small task, so these shout outs will take some time. Please bear with me.

First, I want to give a special thank you to my wife and queen of my universe and empire, Nesheda. We have made history and battled this thing called life together and triumphed. To my children, Sha (the world's greatest dancer and most talented oldest daughter in the world), Brandon (the kindest and most selfless son anyone can ask for and my sidekick), Mo (the funniest and coolest daughter in the world, you are smart but don't get too smart, lol), the twins (my "sonshines"), my sisters Nicola, Dedee, and Keisha, and to my many children in the extended village. Lee, Angelic, Kristen, and all my children, you make me smile when I'm down. I have so many I can't possibly name you all. But know that I love you all the same.

To my mother and father who raised me to greatness, Sellassie Sawyerr Williams (Mom, the judge, and my heart. You make me proud of where I come from, and everything I am is because of you) and Stevenson Williams (Dad, the maestro and first truly great man I knew). I want to thank you for giving me spirituality and an opportunity that changed my life forever and made me the man I am today. Time has proven that everything you taught me was real and taught out of love. Uncle Z, Uncle Ash, Mama Sawyerr, and to my brothers and sister, Stephen, Napo, and Steph, I love you from the bottom of my heart.

To my aunts (I won't name for fear of missing one and getting killed), and my cousins as well. To Sheneva Paz, the female version of me, I don't have to say I love you because you think my thoughts and feel my feelings. But I will anyway, not for you, but for the world to know, I love you and always will.

I must make it a point to mention my ancestors who have transcended this physical existence, Denise C. Shockley (mother), Marilyn Shockley (grand mom) and Dollie Myers (mom) and the entire Myers family. And to my little brother, Randy Amofa, we made it, all the way to the legends and legendary status. We made it. Rhyme in Peace (RIP).

Thank you to Nakia Stokes aka Snow Michele, for always being an inspiration and true friend. You're the embodiment of charisma and ambition. If I could do half as much as you, I would be good.

To the Stamper family, my brother Greg Stamper Jr. I want to say thank you for everything over the years. You are a visionary who foresaw all the great things that would happen to the both of us. I am more than proud of everything you have accomplished, my love to the family and the institution you have built. My love to the entire CSC family. To the entire "Exit US" crew, I send my love, as well as the members of Rahm Nation. You know who you are. I thank you for being a part of the journey and I wish you success in all your endeavors.

I want to thank the elders of the B/ movement, Giovanni Turner my friend for over ten years, and one of the brightest minds I have had the pleasure of knowing. We made history and will continue. Eric Snipe, my brother for life. I appreciate your belief in me. We saw the valley and the mountain top together and you are among the elite emcees whose rhymes never cease to make me smile. Al B Art, my brother from another mother and laugh partner. You are one of the most talented men I know. A true renaissance man who I believe will shake up the world when they catch on.

Jermain Blalock, my brother who I love dearly and argue with like family (because we are). You are an untapped well of greatness the world needs, let your light shine.

To my brother Marcus Thrower, you have and are as much a part of my greatness as the men who have poured into me words of inspiration and encouragement. In fact, I must say, you are the 2nd member of this 2-man band. Thank you for always putting me up on the newest gear and technology, so I could always improve my albums. I thank you for your friendship and continued belief over the years. You are as much a part of my legacy as anyone and I thank you forever.

Shout out to B/ue Robin for your gifts, tenacity, and ambition, I am sure you will do great things. It's just a matter of time. To James Mtume (aka pops, mentor and legend), I love you and thank you for all of the long conversations that inspired and uplifted me over the years. I don't have the words to express my love and appreciation for you, and I am a wordsmith so what does that tell you? All I can say is I love you and the family for life.

Melvin Sharpe (my brother and mentor), I appreciate your patience and belief in me over the years. Your talks about health have been the most valuable conversations I could have had, because after all, what do we have in this life without our health? You are a part of the global village that made me, and you are as important as any musician that ever taught me a note on an instrument, or scholar who taught philosophy, even though we have those talks as well. My man Doc Martin, for saving Hip Hop with the sickest beats out the NYC baybee and your lovely wife Val! Love you family! My Sistah Latioya, the queen of west coast soul. Love ya sis! And Fatima aka Tima or Fatima Amá, squad all day! Thank you for affirming me when I think people are worried about the next move. You are truly talented and special, and I love you. Angel (aka Honey B), thank you for the spiritual conversations queen, I appreciate and love you, you are so gifted; the world will know.

To my big brother Christopher "Play" Martin, man... you have been a constant voice in my head, guiding me toward the pursuit of true success over the hype. Everything, and I mean everything, that you told me about the business came true. I am forever grateful for your friendship, mentorship, and discussions on art, politics, spirituality and the world at large. Thank you for being the first star to believe in me, from the very beginning. You're the man. Thank you to Dexter Wansel for conversations that you may not know have impacted me and changed me for the better. My love and respect to brother William Hart from the Delphonics. Thank you for embracing me before most knew who I was.

To Brother Harold Preston (This is a Pan African, metaphysical, alchemical, spiritual phenomenon). To the Gamble family, Princess Idia, Kenny Gamble, and Caliph, I love you guys for everything your royal family has brought and continue to bring to the culture.

Much love to you B Slade, a genius of epic proportions. There's only one B Slade and my collaborations with you make me know I am a historic figure, not later, but right now, you are that incredible!

I want to say a quick thank you to activist and attorney Michael Coard for sharing your expansive knowledge on the culture of Hip Hop at Temple University's PASEP program where I got to sit in at the Hip Hop 101 classes. A lot of what you taught was instrumental in my development as a teacher. Thank you and brother Yumi Odom for also allowing me at such a young age to teach the course "THE ART OF RAP" (How to emcee), which became the foundation for this book. To my dear friend Dr. Scot Brown aka Doc B. I want to say thank you for pushing me to make this book as proud a moment as the music I create. I respect your willingness to adapt to change in your own journey. You are proof that the renaissance man of the past can exist in modern times and I am blessed to know you. Dr. Kwasi Konadu, I want to thank you for being a part of this incredible spiritual learning experience. This has been a labor of love for our culture and it took patience and vision, both which you demonstrated throughout this entire process. I am glad the stars aligned and placed you in my path.

Love to my girl Chauntè Wayans for your words of wisdom and blind belief in me. I love ya!

And to the fans, you have always shown me love over the years. You are the truth personified! I thank you for being the first to believe, the first to invest, and the first to speak words of encouragement. Before my peers in the music industry, you were there! I hope my work ethic inspires you and teaches you that there are no boundaries as long as you B/.

Lastly, I want to give a special shout out to all the pioneers of Hip Hop who inspired me. All the legends from every era. I studied you and embraced your teachings to the point that some of you feel like family members, even though we never met.

To any of you who I may have missed, I want to remind you that I am a workaholic. This won't be my last book. If I didn't get you on this one, let's shoot for the next.

Much love and B/
O'HENE SAVÁNT

CPSIA information can be obtained
at www.ICGtesting.com
Printed in the USA
FSHW011637050320
67852FS